Booktalking
that works

Jennifer Bromann

Neal-Schuman Publishers, Inc.
New York   London

Published by Neal-Schuman Publishers, Inc.
100 Varick Street
New York, NY 10013

The paper used in this publication meets the minimum requirements of American National Standard for Information Sciences—Permanence of Paper for Printed Library Materials, ANSI Z39.48–1992.∞

This publication was supported in whole or in part by the U.S. Department of Education under the provisions of the Library Services and Construction Act, administered in California by the State Librarian.

Library of Congress Cataloging-in-Publication Data

Bromann, Jennifer.
    Booktalking that works / Jennifer Bromann.
      p. cm. — (teens @ the library series)
    ISBN 1-55570-403-4 (alk paper)
     1. Book talks. 2. Young adults' libraries—Activity programs. 3. Public
libraries—Services to teenagers. 4. Teenagers—Books and reading.
5. Reading promotion. I. Title. II. Series.

Z718.5 .B76 2001
028.5'5—dc21   2001018340

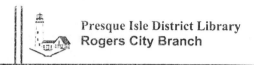

Contents

Part III: Booktalking Resources

Foreword

The *teens @ the library* series pushes us all to broaden our outlook about young adults. Each book in the series strives to show the best practices in individual ways while sharing common goals. Each book will

- Draw from the best, most current research
- Target the changing needs of today's teenagers
- Cite the most innovative models
- Provide real-world-tested practical suggestions
- Call on each of us to aim high

The *teens @ the library* series aims to improve the experience of every young adult with books, libraries, reading, and learning. *Booktalking that Works* by Jennifer Bromann is an energizing interpretation of a classic library tool and breaks new ground.

"Booktalking" is an essentially simple idea: one person talks about specific books to engage a particular audience to read. Although this sounds simple, complexities underlie talking about books to young adults. Successful booktalks can excite teens about reading, encourage them to look for specific titles, search for books by particular authors, and discover books on specific subjects. *Booktalking that Works* is designed to build on this firm foundation and encourages booktalkers to use innovative ways to reach both eager and reluctant teen readers.

Bromann's ideas intrigue me because, like most librarians, I have enjoyed my own experiences as a booktalker. My style grew out of my time as a classroom reading teacher. To immerse my seventh-grade students in the act of reading, I wanted to draw more and more on the library collection and introduce sets of novels to my classroom. I was quite familiar with a great collection of books by an author in our library virtually unknown to most of my students. I brought six or eight books by that author into my classroom and just told the students about them.

Arranging them chronologically, I introduced them like old friends. I tried to convey something about the possible motivation of the author in writing each one as well as what made each title worth reading. I compared the quality and appeal of each book against some of the others, sharing my personal reactions, feeling, insights and responses to the characters and events of the books.

I wish I could tell you that the clouds parted and I looked out on my class to see a rapt audience who fought over the books on the cart. I *can* tell you that over the course of the next week I immediately became aware that something cool was happening. Those books were being checked out and read. And the students who read those books responded to me with their own critiques and then passed the books on to their friends. I had found the part of teaching reading that I liked best—putting the right book into the hands of the right reader at the right time.

I saw interest in reading books multiply. I introduced my students to wonderful authors such as M.E. Kerr, Gary Paulsen, Robin Brancato, Richard Peck, Jeanette Eyerly, Robert Cormier, Paula Danziger, Judy Blume, Robert Heinlein, C.S. Lewis, Catherine Paterson, and Walter Dean Myers in this way. These new books changed my students in different ways. Students already reading proficiently improved their skills, benefited by reading new authors, and grew in their ability to critique and evaluate the quality of what they were reading. I watched excitedly as, one by one, my non-readers became more capable and enthusiastic readers.

I still recall the day a reluctant boy stood at the door to my classroom between classes with Gary Paulsen's *Winterkill* in his hands. In a hushed, awe-filled voice, he confided, "This is the best book I've ever read. Well, really, it's the first book I've ever read all the way through by myself. Does he have any more books that are this good?" It was one of those special moments that teachers and librarians treasure.

My approach to booktalking—and I suspect the approach most readers of this book currently use—is a traditional one. It works well given my personal style and the teen audiences I see, the majority of whom are college bound and generally quite motivated to read. *Booktalking that Works* introduces a fresh approach. The author, Jennifer Bromann is young, bright, and witty. She works as a public librarian in a community where reading challenges to the young adult patrons have demanded an original, dynamic, and resourceful design to booktalking. Her approach builds on all the fundamental tenets of booktalking and enters exciting new areas by adding innovative ideas to proven practices.

What makes teen audiences respond to Bromann's style of booktalks?

Certainly they are much shorter than traditional ones. She talks in the sound bites that today's teens have grown up with and find familiar. She uses techniques that grab their attention by relating the book to their school environment, pop culture, songs, teen movies, and teen TV shows. She demonstrates how to create a booktalking style that is assertive and relevant.

Jennifer Bromann and I agree that there are as many individual approaches to booktalking as there are booktalkers. Our hope is that booktalkers new to the field will discover creative springboards. We trust veteran booktalkers will find new ideas in *Booktalking that Works* to try. If you have not yet taken the plunge into booktalking you might be motivated to start sharing great books with teens in this way. Let me know how it goes. My address is: *shoemaker@iowa-city.k12.ia.us*.

Librarians who booktalk to teens evince a sense of mission about their work. They believe that the right book for the right reader at the right time can be crucial. They strive to make themselves capable, prepared, and ready to make a difference, one teen at a time. *Booktalking that Works* will help us all do just that.

Joel Shoemaker
Series editor

Preface

Many of today's teenagers share one thing in common. They are reluctant readers. Busy teenagers often have the ability to read well but are more interested in movies, music, and electronic games than books. They may be curious about the world of ideas but rarely explore the library. They may think writers and writing are cool but rarely read for pleasure. *Booktalking that Works* offers practical tools to help transform reluctance into excitement.

Today's teens are in some ways different from those of previous generations. This fact explains the need for new approaches, new techniques, and new ideas. While traditional styles are still useful, this book will prepare you to try some completely different approaches. *Booktalking that Works* is designed to get teenagers excited about reading. Teenagers can be a tough audience. They are often afraid to look "un-cool" in front of their peers, and reading is not generally considered to be cool. The booktalker's task is to make it sound like reading these books is "in."

Of course, many students do enjoy reading. They get good grades. They read for fun. They study hard and plan to go to college. They read all the books on the state award list. They read as many of the Accelerated Reader books as they have time for to earn those points. They read all the books in a series. This book is not particularly aimed at serving them. Rather, *Booktalking that Works* offers some practical although radical options which are designed more for the reluctant young adult reader. It is intended especially to help you reach those who don't pay attention in class and who might read only CliffsNotes® or the back of the book for their assignments. It is intended to help you reach those who often might seem to be unreachable. These techniques may not turn all these students into readers, but they will deliver the message that reading and those who read might not be so bad. These students might find that reading reflects their own life for better or worse. They might come to understand that reading can be as entertaining as watching TV or going to the movies. They might even conclude that you, the librarian or teacher, aren't as far out of it as they thought you were.

Booktalking that Works breaks many traditional tenets of booktalking, but it has the same goal as all booktalkers—to foster interest in reading and the library. The ultimate audience for this creative style of booktalking is those attention-spanless, non-reading, wandering-eyed students who respond more to shock or humor and an entertaining delivery than to a smooth, poetic, and grammatically correct literary style. This book may not be for every young adult librarian, but there is something in it for every librarian who serves young adults. Everything in here has worked with real teens. The techniques and booktalks described have been tested in the real world of students, librarians, teens, public libraries, and school libraries.

Booktalking that Works is not only for those who want to improve their booktalks to young adults. It is also for those who have no clue where to begin or what to do. It is for those who can't read a passage dramatically and mesmerize an audience. It is for those who feel that the traditional talks don't fit their style. It is for everyone who has trouble coming up with ways to make books sound interesting. You may never have the nerve to attempt some of the things this book suggests, but you will also find other options that are easy and quick and that anyone can do. For example, it may help you stop spending hours writing long summaries, and instead learn to write short and simple, yet creative and exciting, talks that interest today's young adults.

Part I is devoted to the "how" of booktalking. Chapter 1, "What Teens Want/What Teens Need," identifies and describes the needs of reluctant readers who can be enticed to read with nontraditional approaches. In Chapter 2, "Choosing Books," this theme is specifically applied to the task of finding the best books to talk about. (The Internet is suggested as one interesting new place to get information about books that will work best for teens.) I also talk in Chapter 2 about my experiences in reading and booktalking in specific genres.

Chapter 3, "Techniques," describes the most important considerations regarding what to say (or not say) and how to say it. Chapter 4, "Seven Surefire Booktalking Methods," shows you how to use scene, character, mood, and plot-focused booktalks along with other types of talks, such as those that refer to popular culture, current events, and other real life contexts.

"Preparing Booktalks," Chapter 5, details the process of creating an exciting and useful booktalk, citing many specific examples. One must have audience for booktalks, so Chapter 6, "In the Schools" is about finding, creating, and maintaining links to the teens in schools and public libraries. Part II comprises examples of 50 booktalks and Part III contains supplementary material—Internet resources and a bibliography of other sources of information.

When reading *Booktalking That Works*, please keep the following in mind. Focus on what will work in your community. Are the majority of the high school students college bound? Is reading encouraged in the schools? These factors will affect your approach to the books you choose.

The professional literature about booktalking is dated. Some of the best sources are a decade to more than a half century old, and, although philosophically sound, they do not speak to the changing needs of today's media-savvy, plugged-in teens. Librarians and teens are a varied group. Books one person likes, another person may not like. Did you know there are more than 8,000 books printed for children and young adults of all ages in the United States each year? (Ink and Grabois, 2000 p. 508). With so many books available, each librarian and each teen reader can easily develop a personal repertoire of favorite books to read and talk about.

Booktalking that Works stems from the experiences of a youth librarian in a public library. Although I have taken courses in school media, worked in a school, and have visited many school media centers, most of the situations described directly reflect experiences of a public librarian. Nevertheless, they can certainly be transferred to school libraries and translated to any setting involving teenagers.

Although young adults can range anywhere from 11 to 20 years old, this book focuses on those who are in seventh grade through high school. Many of the suggestions work best for a high school audience.

All teens are different—coming from different communities, with unique interests, cultures, backgrounds, diverse religions, and personal experiences—today's teen readers are likely to have some things in common. The following assumptions about reluctant teen readers guided the writing of this book. Most reluctant young adult readers:

- Are busy
- Are different from one another
- Are more interested in other media than books
- Have a short attention span
- Have the ability to read well
- Don't read for pleasure
- Rarely come to the library
- Prefer lighter, high-interest, and alternative kinds of reading to more traditional genres of literature

Knowing these assumptions, keep an open mind. There are many different views and opinions on books and booktalking. Some support each other while others seem contradictory. There is no exact science to booktalking, just as there is no single, absolute, and perfect way to work with all teenagers. Do not expect to agree with everything in this book. It presents a nontraditional approach to entice the reluctant young adult reader—the teen reader who is the most difficult to reach. Perhaps some of these techniques can also be applied to meet the needs of other readers.

I have always found booktalking to be an exciting and inspiring part of being a YA librarian. I got that first opportunity when I became head of youth services at the Prairie Trails Public Library in Burbank, Illinois. I found the perfect opportunity to start booktalking when the head of the English department at the local high school approached us to help with their reading program. I loved booktalking but none of the booktalks I read in books or online seemed to reflect the booktalking method that worked so well with the teenagers I met. In time, I began to develop my own.

Soon I began to share my experience with teachers and other librarians. I continued reading all the sources on booktalking I could find, and then moved on to literature about teenagers and their reading and other habits. I searched for magazines and Web sites for teenagers that had book reviews and that represented their lifestyle. I planned for workshops, presented more booktalks, and discovered I had many more ideas to share. I quickly found that new ideas keep coming!

Booktalking that Works examines survey results and provides a glimpse of what teenagers read. It shows you different ways to present booktalks. It explores the various genres that work best and how you can use them with young adults. A step-by-step process has been developed to help you write booktalks when you have chosen your books and over 50 examples are included. There are even hints on how to write a booktalk without reading the book. This method is not recommended, but it is something busy librarians in a bind may need to know.

Whether you use one thing, everything, or nothing in this book, I hope that it will at least entertain you and show you something you never thought of before. I hope that it will encourage you to booktalk, and I hope it will help you to understand today's teenagers a little bit better.

REFERENCE

Ink, Gary, and Andrew Grabois. 2000. "Book Title Output and Average Prices: 1998 Final and 1999 Preliminary Figures." In *The Bowker Annual*. New York: R.R. Bowker.

Acknowledgments

I must thank two people first. If Rick Margolis, an editor of *School Library Journal*, had not given me the chance to rewrite the booktalking article I submitted, then Joel Shoemaker would have never offered me the opportunity to write this book. Charles Harmon of Neal-Schuman was also very important in the development of this project.

I would never have had time to complete this project without the help of the Prairie Trails Public Library staff. I offer my special thanks to Ruth Faklis, who gave me the freedom to try new things. Thanks also to Mike Giometti, who located almost all the books and articles and some of the statistics used in this book.

I also thank my family for putting up with all my calls and e-mails asking about wording and grammar. I especially thank my sisters, Natalie Bromann and Valerie Bromann, for helping me with my survey results, movie and grammar questions, and fact checking, and Natalie for helping organize the index. Last, for helping with survey results and for making my life somewhat easier, I thank my teen volunteers.

Part I

Booktalking Techniques

Chapter 1

What Teens Want/
What Teens Need

WHO ARE THESE NEW TEENS ANYWAY?

Teenagers can be seen at the mall, at the movies, at under-21 dance clubs, on the corner, in parking lots, in the woods, in arcades, on friends' porches, in basements and backyards, in late-night restaurants, on their bikes or skateboards, on the football field or basketball court, working at McDonald's™, or cruising in a car or by foot. They are not likely to be found hanging out at the library just for fun. True, teens do come to the library when programs are offered or when they have assignments. There are always a few regulars. Some libraries have large young adult (YA) departments with full-time staff, great collections, and resources that make the library an inviting place for teenagers. School libraries, similarly, may be wonderful facilities that are frequently packed with eager students or students needing assistance with assignments. Typically, though, the majority of teens are not regular users of your average library.

"Many YAs don't want to be in libraries. They are there because they have to be: it is not a matter of choice on their part" (Jones, 1998, p. 29). In 1997 young adults made up 15 percent of the patronage, whereas children made up 33 percent, and adults 52 percent (Dunn, 2000, p. 396). Most teenagers do need a library card to satisfy school requirements. In my community about 12 percent of those entering seventh through ninth grade now participate in the summer volunteer and/or young adult reading program. Before a volunteer program was instituted, however, this number was significantly less. Usage by teenagers also depends on what you and your library has to offer, including technology, resources, space, and programming.

Teenagers have after-school or summer jobs and babysitting, band or choir, sports, television, friends, clubs, lessons, homework, and so on. Not much time for reading for fun, especially when their favorite TV shows are on, or they can run down the block to pick up the latest movie release or even have one delivered to their home. Personal computers and video games beckon from their rooms. They spend time alone crying over lost boyfriends and friends, their parents' divorce, and other teen devastations. True, many teens do read for pleasure, but many more only read what is required for school, if that. Teens spend hours on homework and at jobs and are often practically asleep in their classes. Many teens care for younger siblings after school. In fact, research shows that many teens "feel overwhelmed by pressure and responsibilities" (Kantrowitz and Wingert, 1999, p. 38). When they do so much, are so busy, and have no one demanding that they read, why would they want to read for pleasure?

As beneficial as reading can be for one's intelligence, socializing is necessary too. Wouldn't most people, teens included, opt to go out with friends rather than stay in and read even a great novel? But when they are going on a long trip or need a book for class, when they want something to read before bed or by the pool in the summer, when they are ready to read for any reason whatsoever, that is where we come in.

Many think that the time teenagers spend online and playing video games is a problem that needs to be solved. But these new media experiences help define the new teen, and present opportunities for us to serve their needs. Libraries and librarians will not turn back the world's cultural clock. More technology and fun toys to occupy a teenager's time will appear faster than ever. We will not be able to keep up with them all. Teenagers will continue to wear minimal clothing (except skateboarders) and they will stop playing with dolls at an earlier and earlier age. Many girls are even entering puberty when they are six or seven (Gorman, 2000, p. 84). We have to meet them where they are. They won't give up these things. They live in this culture. But maybe they will read, too, especially if we can stimulate their interest based on what they need or want.

READING: IT'S NOT JUST BOOKS ANYMORE

A person who loves to read may think that video games are a waste of time, or that chat rooms are dangerous places to be avoided, or that the Internet is too time-consuming and objectionable. But Katz asserts in *Geeks: How Two Lost Boys Rode the Internet Out of Idaho* (Katz, 2000, p. xviii) that for some students the Internet is the only place where they can find acceptance, and even develop friendships. This statement may be especially true for boys, and more especially true for those teens who feel rejected by their peers. They feel increased self worth for their skills in hacking. They grow stronger emotionally when they interact with others in games. They develop relationships with people who don't care what they look like or how old they are. They only care about the interests they have in common and how well they present themselves through words. For these teens, don't expect books to beat out the Internet.

After all, if you have searched the World Wide Web recently, you will have noticed that, despite a heavy dose of graphics and easy-to-navigate point-and-click interfaces, the majority of the content or the real information or meaning is still communicated via words. Spending hours on the Internet means spending hours reading. Playing online interactive games is social behavior. Writing e-mail or instant messaging is real, valid, meaningful communication. One of the main points of *Geeks* is to show that at least some of these kids will be getting tomorrow's jobs. The best of this new generation of geeks may prove themselves to be essential to business—without them schools and companies will not run. This idea is something new. It presents them with a whole new world of opportunity and is something to build on with the teens we meet. Let teens know that there is more to reading than books. Reading a novel is no more important than reading the newspaper, a magazine, or a Web site. Reading for information in any form is just as important if not more.

Sally Grant from the Whatcom County Library in Bellingham, Washington, always begins her booktalks by asking classes, "Who doesn't like to read for pleasure?" Sometimes half the class will raise their hands. She proceeds to share other reading with them besides books, such as magazines and *The Pop-Up Book of Phobias*. She suggests "that there are many kinds of 'reading' and a huge variety of 'good stuff' in the library." It may not always satisfy a reading assignment, but lets them know that it is okay if they don't like to read fiction or even nonfiction books. There is other reading out there. Novels are not the only valid form of literature. Multimedia and nontraditional text is also worth promoting. We want to reach out to all readers.

WHAT DO THEY READ (OR NOT READ)?

Teens who don't read for pleasure don't always know there is more be-yond the books they see in school. They often don't know "young adult" or "teen" or "high school" or even "college" books exist. Some school libraries have limited collections because of such factors as low fund-ing, neglect, lack of staff, or inadequate collection development policies. Some public libraries lack YA collections entirely, or "hide" the YA books among the juvenile or adult materials. When a book is needed, teen read-ers tend to go straight from the books taught in grade school and the familiar series books "everyone" was reading to adult titles they hear about from the media and friends. This is what they know. There is noth-ing wrong with that, but they may be missing a section of literature—young adult literature—that is written for them, could be meaningful to them, and could bring them back to books.

Many high school students read adult novels, which is great, but they are often too much of a project when an assignment is due, and they take too much time to read just for pleasure. A teenage student recently said he was going to read John Grisham's *The Firm*, since it was worth 24 points on the Accelerated Reader list. When he discovered how many words were actually on each of the over 400 pages, he opted for *The Westing Game* at eight points instead.

On the other hand, middle school students are often seen reading be-low both their interest or reading level, with books like the *Goosebumps* series by R. L. Stine or classics they've heard about in school like *Charlotte's Web*. They read these books because they are familiar, they've read them before, or they are the only type of book in their school li-brary. Perhaps they've already seen the movie, or it is easy enough to read without working too hard.

Sometimes even YA books may be written at a higher level than some teens, especially those in junior high, are used to or ready for, in terms of maturity or reading skills. In fact, some teens are not yet even ready to read such youth classics as *The Secret Garden*. Once a seventh-grade girl asked me for suggestions about books to read, and I offered all the suggestions I could think of in the youth section, but she claimed to have read them all. When I took her to the YA area she said those books would be too hard for her. She said that she didn't understand them, so we went to the children's section and she selected a book from the new books cart. So it is important to be prepared to provide reading sugges-tions over a wide range of difficulty as well as interest. Teenagers need to be made aware of other possibilities, and librarians must know where to find what they want and how to get those books to them.

TEENS NEED TO RELATE

"Typically, what teens want are books that speak to their experiences, books that talk to them in their language, not down to them." There is a need to "give them what they want, and go to where they are" (Maughan, 1999, p. 28). Booktalks must be presented in a way that shows teens how the books relate to them. If teens are reading about people with the same problems and experiences as themselves, they may actually enjoy what they are reading instead of reading a book just to get through it. Identifying with a book might just give them a more positive attitude about reading, which might encourage them to read more books by the same author, which may then lead to other authors. Getting these books to them is our job, and booktalking is one of the best tools we have to do this job.

According to a survey by the Artists Rights Foundation in Los Angeles and the Boston-based Institute for Civil Society (*www.artistsrights.org/ home.htm*), teenagers say that watching movies is their number one pastime. The survey contacted 600 teens by phone, used focus groups, and studied the activities of 2,000 teenagers in 1998. Results showed that 82 percent of teenagers watch at least one movie in a theatre each month and 87 percent watch one a month at home. Where else can teens go on the weekend that is close to home, that they don't usually need an ID for, and that is not too expensive? "The demographic profile of those who pay full price to see first-run movies (often more than once) is skewed towards those who are old enough to want to meet friends, including those of the opposite sex, at places away from home, but who are not old enough (or rich enough) to go to the restaurants, bars, and clubs" (Bowman, 1999, p. 46)—in other words, teenagers, our target audience. "The number of [television] shows aimed at teens is expected to swell—in record numbers" (Brooke, 1998, p. 18). In fact, entire networks, both cable and broadcast TV, are aimed largely at teens; teen shows can get over two million viewers. Maybe if we want them to read, we have to be ready to give them content as desirable as that in the movies and on TV.

Teens tend to "read about what's hot" (Maughan, 1999, p. 28). Movies and TV spark interest in witchcraft, the *Titanic*, or *Star Wars*, for example. (See the section in this chapter "How Do We Know What We Know" to better assess teen interests.) Look at teenagers' favorite TV

shows and movies to find what you can use to relate the books to them.
Use the same tactics as advertisers. Be a little shifty. Just like studios try
selling the movie to get the money and the ratings, you are selling the
books to get the readers, patrons, or circulation.

KEEPING IN TOUCH

Librarians serving teens, especially those who wish to deliver effective
booktalks to teens, are well advised to keep in touch with the teen world.
It can help to watch their movies and TV shows, listen to their music,
and read their magazines. Teens will listen to you if they think you know
where they are coming from. If you mention Rob Thomas's name, for
example, and a student asks if he is the singer, you should be able to
say, "No, he's not the guy from Matchbox 20, but he was in a band before he became an author." Maybe they'll think that if you know their
music you'll know the books they might like, too. Even if you look like
their mother or father, if you provide biographical details about authors,
at least they might think you have children their age or that you have
similar interests.

Read teen magazines to see what the current interests and trends are.
There are, of course, the old standards for girls like *Teen*, *YM*, and *Sev-
enteen*, but the popularity of magazines is soaring. There are the newer
Twist, *Jump*, *Teen Vogue*, *Girl*, *Girl's Life*, *CosmoGirl*, and *Teen Style*.
Young females often already skip right to such titles as *Cosmopolitan*,
Glamour, *Vogue*, and *Jane*, geared toward twenty-somethings or older.
For guys there are *Transworld Stance* and *MH-18*, and also *Joey* for gay
and bisexual male teenagers. *Bop* and *Teen Beat* still cover entertainment. *Teen People*, *Entertainmenteen*, and *Teen Movieline* are great for
keeping up on the young stars. There are certainly many more that teens
are interested in, but titles above are specifically geared toward this age
group and don't have a limited focus. They are a great way to learn what
interests your teenagers in general. Magazines wouldn't sell if they didn't
appeal to their audiences' interests. They are bright, hip, current, and
topical. Use magazines to help relate to reluctant teen readers. An added
benefit for librarians is that if you read these magazines you can spend
less time listening to their music and watching their TV shows and movies.

A PLACE OF THEIR OWN

When a booktalk is over, don't stop with the last book. Take a minute or two more to tell them where they can find the books in the library. A Houston Public Library Teen Read Week Survey from 1999 (*www.hpl.lib.tx.us/youth/teenreadweek.htm*) showed that next to friends, browsing the library is the second most popular way that 1,636 teens found out about books. Don't reshelve the books and expect that they will find them. Ideally a public library has a YA collection of books, music, magazines, and computers in a separate, comfortably furnished space, a full-time YA specialist, and an active YA advisory board. If you are in a school library, a paperback book rack or place to house new fiction is desirable to get the attention of teenagers. Lacking that, create a place for them to find "their" books, even if it is just a shelf or special bookends. Some public libraries shelve YA books with adult or juvenile books, but maybe an old magazine/book rack can be pressed into service with a "Teen Books" sign above it. Thus you will promote these books to teens who may not otherwise look for them, and many more young adult books will circulate. Of course you can only do as much as space or funding allows, but it is important to take even such small steps. If you wait until everything is perfect and you have established the YA program of your dreams, you are likely never to get started. Advocate for teens in small ways and build the clientele.

We may prepare the best booktalks possible, but the teens still have to come to us to get the books. I recently asked a group of seventh- and eighth-grade volunteers what would make teenagers want to come to the library. Answers included food, free shoes, a Sony Playstation™, an arcade, and a big screen TV. While their replies were obviously not entirely serious, since they know we could never provide all these things, such answers do make a serious point. The only way most teenagers will come to the library is if it has what they like to do, or if it has the books and magazines to let them read about what they do. One girl in my volunteer program said, "Teens don't go to the library." I said "You're all here," and she replied, "But it is for a reason." So maybe the answer is that they secretly would be willing to come to the library, but we have to offer more experiences like volunteering for them to feel they have a purpose there.

WHERE DO THEY LEARN ABOUT BOOKS?

Teens learn about books from magazine reviews, librarians and teachers, the Internet, or browsing the store or library shelves, but, according to surveys, the most popular way for teens to identify books to read is through their friends. The key then is to get to those friends first, so they can spread the word about great books. During summer reading programs, teens tend to check out books their friends just returned, that their friends recorded on their reading logs, or that their friends were talking about. There is no better endorsement of quality than by a friend. People usually form relationships because they have similar interests. They look for their friends' approval of what they read as well as what they wear and what they listen to on the radio. In the teen years especially, people often try to look and act like one another, perhaps adding a touch of individuality to that similar look. That is why so many young people shop at the same stores—why fashions go in and out of style.

For many teens, however, their "style personality is a work in progress, flip-flopping from week to week, from mainstream to extreme" (Bonnell, 2000, p. 155). They change hair color, style, and clothing like veritable chameleons. One mother recently described her two daughters as polar opposites: one wears pajamas to school and the other will only wear something if five other girls already own the same thing. Their book habits are similarly diverse. One may want only books about wolves and another may only want to read the Sweet Valley High series. If they read on their own, some teens want only the books that everyone is talking about just as they want to have the same clothes and listen to the same music. Other teens refuse to conform and will read something more obscure or nothing at all.

WHY BOOKTALK TO TEENAGERS?

Booktalking can motivate and entertain readers. Nonreaders may be inspired to become readers. Those who already read may be exposed to new or different genres in which they may develop an interest. Excellent readers and even reluctant readers may find titles or authors who will challenge and extend their reading tastes. These may be the most common reasons for booktalking to young adults by librarians. But booktalking can also serve many other purposes. One might want to:

- Highlight new titles or special collections
- Introduce a new or particular series or genre or author

- Offer books on a theme or topic of interest or relevance
- Help students meet particular curricular objectives
- Build public library and school relationships and cooperation
- Establish readers' advisory relationships between students and librarians
- Strengthen ties with schools, school librarians, and teachers
- Enhance community relations (Shoemaker, 2000)

Middle school is "the age when we start losing them to adult books both in and out of school, and also the age when we start losing them as readers altogether" (November, 1998, p. 775). This is the age when we need to get them back. Of course, there are many seventh and eighth graders, and even some high school students, who browse the new bookshelves and anxiously wait for the latest book in a series. We think we are doing well when we see that, but these students will read on their own anyway. Maybe their parents started them on it, or perhaps they were motivated by a TV show, a teacher, a librarian, or a friend. But so many other teens never even come to the library, or they don't come until the end of the semester when they realize they won't graduate without handing in a satisfactory report or completing required public service hours.

If the first goal of this book is to get teens who don't read to do so, an important subgoal is to show teens that maybe reading and books aren't as weird and un-cool as they may have thought. An important part of that effort is to deliver booktalks that engage and entertain the audience, so that, if nothing else, they are left with a positive attitude about books and libraries. The goal of booktalking is not necessarily to sell particular books as much as it is to sell the idea of reading. The point is to leave every listener with a good impression of books and the library, even if they never pick up a book you tell them about. Booktalking is not about *making* them read. When book report time comes around, however, students may be looking for that book they vaguely remember hearing about.

A SHORT HISTORY OF BOOKTALKING

In *Keep Talking That Book! Booktalks to Promote Reading Volume II* Carol Littlejohn notes that there is no known inventor of booktalking (Littlejohn, 2000, p. 1). It certainly seems likely that anyone presenting books to children, young adults, and adults, as far back as books have been available, gave booktalks. Librarians telling children about *Little*

Women, by Louisa May Alcott, and *The Adventures of Huckleberry Finn,* by Mark Twain, were giving informal booktalks.

Perhaps one of the oldest sources available mentioning the actual art form of booktalking is Amelia H. Munson's *An Ample Field* (Munson, 1950, pp. 97–101). However, in *The Fair Garden and the Swarm of Beasts,* Margaret Edwards discusses performing booktalks in the 1930s when it was difficult to get into Baltimore schools (Edwards, 1994, pp. 31–32).

Joni Bodart has done the most research and published the most on the subject of booktalking to date. Many others (such as Mary Kay Chelton, John Gillespie, Diane Lembo, Patrick Jones, Nancy Keane, Nancy Polette, John Sexton, Anne Guevara, Kathleen A. Baxter, Marsha Agness Kochel, Terrence David Nollen, Gail Reeder, and Hazel Rochman) have also published in the field, making it a growing and changing part of youth librarianship. As long as teenagers continue to have different interests and fads, and as long as writers write new books, booktalking will always have a need for change, yet will never break too far away from the tradition and goals of the people who saw its beginning.

HOW DO WE KNOW WHAT WE KNOW?

It is important to look at recent surveys and statistics regarding teenagers and their reading interests to see what *they* want. Of course, it is important to note that most teenagers answering these surveys are already readers, as the surveys are usually offered on sites where readers go, such as library Web pages or other literary or teen sites. Each survey offers different genre alternatives, so it is difficult to compare the same data across several surveys. Nevertheless, some commonalities can be found. It is also important to note that online surveys are rarely monitored. No one can legitimately check a respondent's gender or age, and they often can't detect multiple responses. It is even possible that some crafty librarians or other adults are getting in there to alter results or relive their teenage years.

The purpose of each survey is different, and although some of the conclusions are also different, many are the same. It is interesting, for example, that mystery, horror, and adventure were the top three choices in several surveys asking for favorite genres. Survey results also seem to suggest that, while teenagers often want to read or enjoy reading, they do not read often and they do not choose it as a favorite activity over other choices listed on the survey. Finally although there are flaws with every survey, something can be learned from each one.

SmartGirl.com Survey

The SmartGirl.com (*www.SmartGirl.com*) survey was conducted during Teen Read Week in October 1999 for the Young Adult Library Services Association (YALSA), a division of the American Library Association (ALA), on the SmartGirl.com Web site. Since many teenagers who frequent SmartGirl.com may not necessarily be readers, this survey's results may give a closer view than other surveys of what teenage girls and boys really read. It still must be considered that it was not a random survey, but only a survey of those young people, mostly girls, who visited SmartGirl.com during this time period. They may have been encouraged by teachers or librarians to visit the site or they may have discovered it on their own.

According to the survey, almost half the respondents claimed they don't have much time to read for pleasure, but they like to read when they get the chance. Half the girls and 32 percent of the boys said they read "Just for the fun of it," while only 19 percent said they read because they have to for school. In order from most popular to least, their top interests in books were:

- Mystery
- Adventure
- Horror
- True stories
- Fantasy
- Science fiction
- Romance
- Sports
- Nonfiction

Since 55 percent said they prefer to read about people or characters like themselves, these teens must go on adventures, see ghosts, and live fantastical lives. Or maybe they just want the characters to be real yet magical or adventurous like Harry Potter from J. K. Rowling's books—someone they can relate to. However, they also indicated that they like to read about celebrities.

When asked to report what their favorite books were, young adults tended to choose a series author, popular adult author, or a book often required in school. That tendency doesn't necessarily mean that they don't or would not like traditional YA books or other adult books about teenage or twenty-something characters. It may just mean that there are too many books for a favorite to be determined. It may also mean that some authors or titles are more likely to come to mind while completing an online survey.

It is fun to check out the many surveys on different topics on this Web site. True, respondents are mostly SmartGirl.com frequenters, but their answers still give ideas of what is new in the teen world, even if it is not necessarily the views of all teenagers.

Houston Public Library Survey

The Houston Public Library reading survey from 1999 recorded responses from 825 males and 811 females. An online survey was conducted. In addition, Patrick Jones, the creator, reports that a print survey was distributed and returned at libraries and school libraries and "hand" surveys were conducted during Teen Read Week booktalks (Jones, 2000).

In this survey the majority favored reading magazines, with books in second place, comic books third, and newspapers last. They prefer fiction to nonfiction, and once again, horror, mystery, and adventure scored high.

As for fiction, the genres they chose are as follows:

Types of Fiction	Number of Votes
Horror	504
Mystery	339
Adventure	288
Teen Problems	258
Sports	246
Humor	239
Fantasy	217
Romance	204
Historical Fiction	175
Science Fiction	114
Classics	58
Graphic Novels	54

As for nonfiction this is what they liked best:

Favorite Nonfiction Books	Number of Votes
Music/TV/movies	659
True crime	332
Sports	304
Poetry	214
History	164
Biography	129
Science	99
Health	69

How do they find out about new books? Mostly from friends. Next, the most frequent method is by browsing the library. Third was from asking librarians, followed by browsing the store, finding out from teachers, hearing about them on TV, checking amazon.com, and reading reviews.

The SmartGirl.com and Houston Public Library surveys indicate that the most popular reading choices are mystery, adventure, and horror. Each teenager is an individual, but teens overall have universal likes and dislikes as well as similar experiences. Putting these trends and tendencies to work to promote reading and libraries is what librarians serving youth need to do best. Would the teens in your library respond with the same interests as those in Houston? A short survey might provide an answer.

Prairie Trails Public Library Survey

The following results were obtained from a survey of over 300 teenagers in my community of Burbank, Illinois, during April 2000. A survey of your own teen population might serve you the best. This one was a bit long. The students actually wanted to finish the questionnaire despite having it ripped out of their hands by teachers and student collectors as time ran short. This eagerness to respond may simply indicate that they preferred writing about themselves to learning about the Dewey Decimal System or how to use the card catalog, but most respondents appeared to answer honestly and their answers were helpful.

Survey results can be confusing to interpret. Some middle school students marked "hate" as the phrase that best describes how they feel about reading, yet, inexplicably, they still marked many of the genre selections listed on the survey as being things they "like to read about." Some respondents only filled out one side of the survey and never turned it over to complete the other side. There seemed to be a "word-of-mouth" effect in that many in the same class indicated that they liked the same book. So, although it is clear that not all survey results can be trusted as completely accurate, a simple survey that is locally created, administered, and interpreted can certainly help you make better selection and collection development decisions. Just as important, survey results can be used to help build support for increased resources, additional services, and the like. Here is what the seventh and eighth graders who took this survey selected as the books they "like to read about":

Subject	Number of Teenagers Responding
Scary/horror	240 (65%)
Mysteries	195 (53%)
Love/romance	183 (50%)
Teen/YA	172 (47%)
True stories	146 (40%)
Sports	132 (36%)
Friends	118 (32%)
Dating	105 (28%)
Science fiction	102 (27%
Fantasy	101 (27%)
Adult	100 (27%)
Short stories	97 (26%)
Graphic novels	73 (20%)
Classics	44 (11%)
School	34 (9%)

It is not surprising that scary books ranked highest given the popularity of horror films with teenage characters. It is also not surprising to see mysteries up there, since that category is popular in most surveys.

Many more questions (too many, in fact) were asked, such as "What is your favorite TV show?" "What is the last movie you saw?" and "What is your favorite book or author?" The majority of responses to this last question was *The Outsiders*, by S. E. Hinton, which just happens to be required reading in the junior high and the last book they read. The other questions prompted too diverse a set of responses to be meaningful. What did I learn? Surveys are tricky, but a short, clear, simple one can quickly and easily produce much useful information.

Bruno & Ridgeway Survey

Bruno & Ridgeway conducted a survey for *Publishers Weekly* and BookExpo America in June of 1998. The survey not only included interviews of adults, but also 100 teens who had purchased a book in the last three months. One must consider of course that the interviewees are readers, since they could only take the survey if they had purchased a book. The survey included 53 girls and 47 boys ages 12 to 17. The majority felt that "reading is a lot of fun, is cool and is something that makes them feel smarter than people who don't read" according to the results published in *Publishers Weekly* (Ferguson, 1998, p. 30). Of those who responded, 72 percent said they bought their last book for fun and not for school (although the survey was conducted in the summer when they have no schoolwork and are not required to purchase materials for school). They preferred fiction by 57 percent and 75 percent said they preferred books in a series. When asked what types of books they like best, they chose the following:

- Mysteries (50%)
- Science fiction and fantasy (41%)
- Books about celebrities and athletes (36%)
- How-to books (26%)

When questioned about their use of other media, responses reveal something different:

Media	% of Boys	% of Girls
Watching TV	62%	36%
Playing tapes/CDs/records	57%	74%
Listening to the radio	49%	77%
Playing computer/video games	43%	13%
Talking on the telephone	38%	64%
Surfing the Internet	28%	23%
Reading for fun	9%	25%

When given other choices, reading doesn't seem as "cool" and "fun" as they previously claimed. Maybe if there were no video games the boys would score reading higher. It is also interesting to see a distinct difference in the preferences of boys and girls (note the phone and video game usage and reading habits).

How do these teens choose books? The majority makes selections from reading or viewing the front or back cover.

Teenage Research Unlimited Surveys

Teenage Research Unlimited (*www.teenresearch.com*) conducts two studies a year for marketing purposes. In the fall of 1998 selected teenagers ages 12 to 19 chose the top five things they talk about with their friends in the *TRU Teenage Marketing and Lifestyle Study*. Their choices are as follows:

- Boyfriend/girlfriend (38%)
- Other friends (36%)
- Life in general (35%)
- Someone you want to go out with (35%)
- Music (30%)
- Sex (27%)
- Gossip (26%)
- The future (25%)
- Next weekend (25%)
- Last weekend (23%)
- Movies/TV shows (21%)
- Sports (21%)
- Secret stuff (20%)
- Current events (19%)
- School/grades (18%)
- Jobs (16%)
- Deep feelings (15%)
- College (12%)
- Fashion (12%)
- Video games/computers (11%)
- Parents (9%)
- Celebrities (7%)
- Vacations (6%)
- Brother/sister (4%)
- Your attitude (4%)
- Your behavior (3%)
- Eating habits (2%)

Keep in mind that these were the total results for boys and girls surveyed. Females, for example, rated fashion and deep feelings higher than males, and males rated video games and sports higher than females. Interestingly, books was not one of the choices. These results are used to advertise to teens, so why not use them to advertise books to teens? Why not use them to present and write books on subjects teenagers talk about? Such information can help us focus on the interests of teens. If they discuss these things with friends then they would most likely prefer to read about these things. Furthermore, these are the hooks we need to use in booktalking.

REFERENCES

Artists Rights Foundation. 2000. *www.artistsrights.org/home.htm*.

Bonnell, Kim. 2000. "Wear and When." *The Look: In Style* (Fall): 15.

Bowman, James. 1999. "Ain't Gettin' Any Older." *National Review* 51 (November 8): 46.

Brooke, Jill. 1998. *Adweek* (February 2): 19.

Dunn, Christina. 2000. "Assessment of the Role of School and Public Libraries in Support of Educational Reform: Final Report on the Study." In *The Bowker Annual*, 45th ed. Edited by Dave Bogart. New Providence, N.J.: R. R. Bowker.

Edwards, Margaret. 1994. *The Fair Garden and the Swarm of Beasts: The Library and the Young Adult*. Chicago: American Library Association.

Ferguson, Amanda. 1998. "Reading Seen as Cool." *Publishers Weekly* 245 (October 12): 28–31.

Gorman, Christine. 2000. "Growing Pains." *Time* 156 (August 21): 84.

Grant, Sally. YALSA-BK: 12337. *www.ala.org/yalsa/professional/yalsalists.html* (November 21, 2000).

Houston Public Library. 1999. Houston Public Library Teen Read Week Survey. *www.hpl.lib.tx.us/youth/teenreadweek.htm*.

Jones, Patrick. 1998. *Connecting Young Adults and Libraries: A How-To-Do-It Manual*, 2d ed. New York: Neal-Schuman.

Jones, Patrick. 2000. Survey. E-mail *bromannj@hotmail.com* from *Naughyde@aol.com* (September 28, 2000).

Kantrowitz, Barbara, and Pat Wingert. 1999. "How Well Do You Know Your Kid?" *Newsweek* 133 (May): 36–40.

Katz, Jon. 2000. *Geeks: How Two Lost Boys Rode the Internet Out of Idaho*. New York: Villard Books.

Littlejohn, Carol. 2000. *Keep Talking That Book!: Booktalks to Promote Reading Volume II*. Worthington, Ohio: Linworth Publishing.

Maughan, Shannon. 1999. "Making the Teen Scene." *Publishers Weekly* 246 (October 18): 28–31.

Munson, Amelia H. 1950. *An Ample Field: Books and Young People.* Chicago: American Library Association.

November, Sharyn. 1998. "Field Notes: I'm Not a Teenager— I Just Read Like One." *Horn Book* 74 (November/December): 775.

Shoemaker, Joel. Conversation with Jennifer Bromann. February 2000.

SmartGirl.com and the American Library Association. 2000. SmartGirl.com survey. *www.SmartGirl.com.*

Teenage Research Unlimited. 1998. TRU Teenage Marketing and Lifestyle Study. *www.teenresearch.com.*

BOOKS FOR TEENS MENTIONED IN THIS CHAPTER

Alcott, Louisa May. 1868. *Little Women.*

Burnett, Frances Hodgson. 1909. *The Secret Garden.*

Greenberg, Gary. 1999. *The Pop-Up Book of Phobias.* New York: Rob Weisbach Books.

Grisham, John. 1991. *The Firm.* New York: Doubleday.

Hinton, S. E. 1967. *The Outsiders.* New York: Viking Press.

Raskin, Ellen. 1978. *The Westing Game.* New York: Dutton.

Twain, Mark. 1884. *The Adventures of Huckleberry Finn.*

White, E. B. 1952. *Charlotte's Web.*

Chapter 2

Choosing Books

Booktalks should reflect the audience, their needs, and their interests. Remember that you are trying to make reading fun—your audience should not feel that it is an assignment. You are probably not there to educate them about any particular subject, but to "sell" them on the idea of reading in general and make them aware of some good books.

Choosing books is just as important as the booktalks themselves since you want to make sure that you "sell" books that your audience will finish reading. The best way to choose a good book for a general booktalk is to decide if it has appeal to this age group. Does it have boy/girl relationships, sex, friendships, aliens, ghosts or witches, drugs, danger, murder, scheming? Does it reflect the popular genre choices reflected in the surveys? What books on amazon.com sell best? Which books get the best reviews by YAs? What books do you see in teen magazines or Web sites? Generally, popular movies, TV shows, and magazines are a clue to current interests. You might want to check what circulates best in your library or consult online surveys, identify best-selling books, and consider what you hear teens talking about or see them doing. Consult YALSA's many fine lists of books (*www.ala.org/yalsa/booklists/*). True, each teen has individual tastes, interests, and needs, but it is important to identify overall current interests and fads and use those in the booktalks.

WHERE TO FIND BOOKS TEENS WILL WANT TO READ

Journals and Magazines

Traditionally journals have been the best source for book selection. But with teen sections in bookstores or their online counterparts, Web sites for teenagers, book lists by librarians, and magazines, there are more options than ever for choosing the best books for young adults.

Print reviews appear in *The Bulletin of the Center for Children's Books*, *Booklist*, *Kliatt*, *Voice of Youth Advocates*, *School Library Journal*, *Horn Book*, *Publishers Weekly*, *CCBC Choices*, and other traditional library publications. Still, these sources primarily present the opinions of current or former librarians, teachers, or other academic or book professionals who may or may not have knowledge and up-to-date expertise about today's teens. In other words, their recommendations may or may not reflect the real needs of teens.

Some of the best sources to find out what teens are reading or might be interested in reading are the magazines they buy and the Web sites they visit. For example, 68 percent of teen males and 81 percent of teen females indicated that they had read a magazine for pleasure in the "last week" according to the "Teenage Marketing Lifestyle Study" (Harvey, 2000, p. 33). Teens are more likely to come to the library looking for items recommended by a friend or specific titles mentioned, excerpted, reviewed, or featured in a magazine they read and like. The online versions of many of these magazines or Web sites geared toward teenagers give teens the opportunity to write and share their own reviews for the books. For some, this feature may be a chance to test a career dream. For others, it might be fun to see their names in print, and know that other people will read what they have to say. For whatever reason, many teens find such interactivity empowering and they enjoy posting their opinions. Use their opinions to help make selections for others.

Unfortunately magazines and sites for boys with book reviews are relatively rare. Nevertheless, there are a great many magazines that interest boys. Guys seem to request and check out magazines geared toward one particular interest, such as *WWF*, *Transworld Skateboarding*, *Sports Illustrated*, *Ride BMX*, and *Gamepro*.

Most specialty magazines do not offer book reviews. If they do, they are on the same subject as the magazine. Most beauty/fashion magazines do have reviews for girls. Many of the books reviewed on these "girl" sites and in these "girl" magazines are about guys too, so for the librarian looking for contemporary books for booktalks, these reviews are still relevant. Figure 2.1 is a list of magazines with Web sites that offer book reviews for teenagers. As previously stated, the reviews are mostly for girls. Also, in only a year, many of the magazines changed their format, eliminating, adding, moving, or only occasionally running book reviews.

An extra benefit of these sites and magazines is that they not only help you identify books that might be popular for teenagers, but they also reveal other topics that interest them. It is easier than ever to find books and hooks for booktalking.

Figure 2.1
Popular Teen Magazines with Online Versions
that Offer Book Reviews

Magazine, Catalog, or Magalog	Online Magazine Counterpart
Entertainmenteen. No reviews, but new "book releases" are listed on the same page as new movie and CD releases. This is great because teens see what's new in books in the same place they see what's new in other media.	They say Web site will be coming soon.
Girl. Reviews books mostly about African American characters or real people.	*www.girlzine.com* This site does not contain book reviews, although it is fun to read occasional comments by girls about the books they like or don't like.
Girls' Life. Many book reviews for younger teens. Librarians' favorites.	*www.girlslife.com* Book section online features different books from magazine.
Jane. More for twenty-somethings, but that is always an appeal for high school, and even younger, readers. Sometimes they review subjects that won't be of interest to most teenagers, such as travel.	*www.janemag.com* If you look hard enough you can find book reviews, but the books often have mature content.
Joey. Most of the reviews are on books about gay or bisexual characters. A good source to find those titles when needed, especially when there is a collection of short stories where one or a few of the stories are about homosexual characters.	*www.joeymag.com* Web site does not contain book reviews.

Figure 2.1(cont.)

Jump. Sometimes has book reviews.

www.jumponline.com No reviews.

MH-18. Books included generally appeal to male characters.

www.mh18.com No book reviews at this time.

Seventeen. Offers reviews for new books geared to teens or adult books for young adults. Some are not on the Web site. They often feature books, especially popular nonfiction that you may not see reviewed in other places. Book reviews are on same page as movie reviews.

www.seventeen.com Several books are reviewed, although only one is featured each month. More reviews are offered online than in the magazine. Members who join free can rate and discuss books with others who have read them.

Teen. Includes book reviews in the "What's Up" section.

www.teenmag.com Lists top 10 books chosen by the people at *teenmag.com.* Teens can submit a book review and the best will be chosen to add to the site.

Teen People Book Club. This catalog comes to you once you join, and to join you only have to buy one book for $2.95, plus shipping and handling. The catalogs include book reviews from actual teenagers.

www.teenpeoplebookclub.com Even if you don't join, you can view descriptions of books online. They do a great job of selecting books geared toward teenagers, especially adult books. Teen reviews included online as well.

Teen Voices. Teens review books.

www.teenvoices.com No book reviews available online.

Transworld Stance. A lifestyle magazine aimed at male teenagers, with sports, fashion, entertainment, and girls. It has book and e-zine reviews, too, with a mix of fiction and nonfiction.

No Web site at this time.

It seems more magazines are available for teenagers today than in any other generation. Of course, who knows how long some of these magazines will last? Magazines are and always have been ephemeral. Like Web sites, they come and go as trends do.

The Internet

Today the Internet is probably the best source to find books to booktalk and to identify the interests of teenagers. The Cheskin Research and Cyberteen survey (*www.cheskin.com/think/studies/netteens.html*) found that a "majority of teens (55%) consider the Web better than watching TV. Instead of preferring to be passively entertained, teens are exploring, interacting and creating" (Cheskin Research, 1999). Teens are checking e-mail, reading online magazines, searching for information on their favorite stars, chatting, downloading music, and doing research for school. So naturally we will now find more information on teen books and interests from these sources as well.

Although it is important and often required in selection policies to check reviews, the Internet provides a variety of options for determining what the teenager wants instead of what the librarian/reviewer wants. When you are in immediate need of finding books for a booktalk or when you want to see what is popular, the Internet is the way to get started today.

Jobbers with CD-ROM or online selection/ordering tools often provide citations for published reviews or links to them. If a title you are considering for purchase has not yet been reviewed in the professional journals you use, electronic tools can help you locate other reviews. Online bookstore sites also provide some professional reviews, as well as reader responses.

The Internet is where many teens are finding their books, so librarians should be attentive to this option. Here you are likely to read about new books, including some that you might never identify using traditional print versions of the professional review sources. Bookstore sites, for example, often market books before they are reviewed anywhere else.

Instead of spending money on print subscriptions to magazines, teens can now go to the Internet for online versions of their favorite magazines, or they can go to e-zines specifically created for the Internet. Figure 2.2 is a selected list of Web sites and e-zines not affiliated with a print magazine. Their focus is on teenagers, and they include book reviews. There are, of course, many more sites out there. As some disappear, others will no doubt appear; that is a reflection of the constant state of change in the world of the World Wide Web. But there will always be similar sites as more and more teens gain access to computers in their

Figure 2.2
Web Sites or E-zines
Offering Book Reviews for or About Teens

Web Sites	What the Site Contains
www.Teenreads.com	Many book reviews not by teenagers, listed by authors as well as features.
http://tln.lib.mi.us/~amutch/jen/index Reading Rants	Jennifer Hubert, a middle school librarian in New York, has great book lists updated with new fiction. Includes many books for older teens.
www.amazon.com	Requires some effort to find their "teens" section. Offers books that are bestsellers on their site. Amazon always lets anyone write a review for books, too, so it is sometimes interesting to see what teenagers think of the young adult books. Various subjects.
www.barnesandnoble.com	It is rumored that teen focus groups help Barnes and Noble select books for this age group. Includes top 10 and editors' picks. Must start in the "Kids!" section, though.
www.SmartGirl.com	Teenagers who fill out a book review form review all books. It is obvious that those books with many reviews are the most popular. Teens also give their age. Any book is eligible.
www.ala.org/teenhoopla	Teens top 10. Submit a book review. Nominate a book for one of YALSA's book lists. All reviews are by teens. More than one review for some books.

Figure 2.2 (cont.)

www.grouchy.com/angstbooks.html Favorite Teenage Angst Books	By Cathy Young, a freelance writer, critic, and Web developer. Books listed by various subjects.
www.borders.com	Listed under "Young Adult" which may not be a familiar or meaningful term to teens, the intended audience. Includes staff picks, popular series, nonfiction, bestsellers, new releases, and fiction.
www.teencybercenter.org	No book reviews, but book lists with titles on specific genres, as well as books purchased monthly by the YA librarian Beth Gallaway who created and maintains the site for Haverhill Public Library, Haverhill, Mass.
www.clpgh.org/ein/ya/yalists.html Carnegie Library of Pittsburgh's Young Adult Booklists	Brief descriptions of books, but broken up into many categories. Useful if you ever need to talk about a book on a specific subject.
www.girlzone.com	Many book reviews by teens divided by levels: Jr.high, Sr.high, and "in other words," which seems to focus on nonfiction. New and old books, for young and old teens.
http://rms.concord.k12.nh.us/ booktalks/ Booktalks—Quick and Simple	Nancy Keane's site does not have book reviews, but booktalks. You can get an idea of what other librarians, teachers, and students are talking about.
www.teenzworld.com	Features YA or adult books for young adults with reviews from amazon.com. Still, they might not see these reviews elsewhere.

homes, at school, in public libraries, and in such other venues as Internet cafes. Sites that would mostly be of use to librarians are also included, as these are useful in selecting books of interest to teenagers.

It is wise to check another source for reviews occasionally in addition to the review journals you regularly see. You may be surprised by what is there and what teens will miss if you don't provide the reading material they encounter in the media.

Consider the following important outcomes of this increased interactive/Internet presence:

- Teen or adult books with teen appeal seem to be gaining more popularity because of Web sources. Many sites blur the lines between books published for adults and teens.
- Several sites allow teens to share their views of a book. They can feel like a book reviewer and that their opinion of the book matters. They now have a forum for their reading opinions.
- When books are featured in magazines or on Web sites—even sometimes on the same page as the latest and coolest music, clothes, movies, and celebrities—the underlying message is that maybe books are cool too. It makes them appear as "valid" as other media. That's an important message to deliver via booktalks, too.

BOOKTALKING CONSIDERATIONS FOR VARIOUS GENRES

In planning a booktalk there may be some topics to avoid. Some books will have limited appeal, while others might prove vastly popular with a huge number of teens. The following considerations for a number of genres or subjects may help you decide what will work best for you, your audience, and your community. This is not meant to be a comprehensive study of each genre and its books, but it provides examples and offers a case for why some genres do or do not work better with teenagers, especially reluctant readers. For a more complete look at the definitions of genres and their examples, read *Teen Genreflecting* (Herald, 1997).

Classics

"There is no doubt that the classics represent man's finest use of language; but it is also true that classic literature is one of the most difficult, most subtle, and most mature expressions of human beings, so it is no surprise that an understanding and enjoyment of the classics comes, if at all, fairly late in a reader's growth" (Carlsen, 1980, p.149). Classics are the books that make reluctant teen readers hate reading. Avoid them when booktalking to high school students and younger—they get these in school anyway. Teenagers tend to dislike anything they are forced to read but cannot understand. When trying to get teens to read, you have to let them know you know what they want, not what some might label "good" or "best" for them.

If the teens in your audience are average readers, and you make *Wuthering Heights* as the most fascinating mystery and romance or if you present *Moby-Dick* as the perfect adventure, they may never trust you—especially when they can't keep their eyes open through all the whale descriptions. In their opinion, you have just moved to the dark side. See their ratings of classics in the surveys—all at or near the bottom. After all, what are they most likely to choose at the video store, horror and comedy films or period films? Even if they liked the recent movie *Sense and Sensibility* when someone else made them watch it, on their own most will pick the teen, horror, or comedy films. Studios know that teenagers spend their money on movies. Many horror and teen films gross from $40 million to over $100 million. True, the 1997 movie *William Shakespeare's Romeo and Juliet* was included in those numbers, but those teen girls went for Leonardo DiCaprio, not for William Shakespeare.

Once they get to love or like reading, or even just not hate it, they will eventually find their way to the classic novels, adult books, and the entire range of literary options. If you have been booktalking to the same group for years, if you know your readers, or if you have been informed of their capabilities by their teachers, then you will be able to determine the mix of books you can present. You might follow the example of Hazel Rochman, who attempts to "push the audience a little beyond where they might want to go on their own" (Rochman, 1987, p. 3). Try to add some adult reads, but choose contemporary ones with issues teens can relate to or are interested in.

Sports

The obvious choice for males is usually sports, but many boys would much rather play or attend a sporting event than read a fictionalized account of it. Many contemporary "sports" books also focus on other issues. For example, in *Necessary Roughness* the characters deal with prejudice and relationships in a new school, and in *Painting the Black* the decision of truth over fame is a factor, widening the appeal to young adults. Choose books with elements of the sport as well as life problems.

Girls are increasingly into sports, and more and more good books focus on women's sports. Most titles are nonfiction by or about popular and contemporary women athletes. Fiction titles are rare for teenage girls, but they include *Offsides* and *The Necessary Hunger: A Novel*. There are now more books about real women's teams that make it to the top, like *The Beautiful Game: Sixteen Girls and the Soccer Season That Changed Everything*, *Soccer Girls*, and *In These Girls, Hope Is a Muscle*.

When booktalking, remember that if you talk mostly about the plays and sporting aspects of the book, those who daydream during a football game or take a snack break during every inning of a baseball game are going to tune you out. Include some comments about other aspects of the book, such as friends and relationships, to broaden its potential appeal. Don't assume that you have to include sports books to make your selections more appealing for both genders. Stereotyping all boys as being interested in sports is just as bad as stereotyping all girls as liking romances. Each teen is unique. Use books about sports, but be careful not to bore the audience with too much detail of the game.

Historical Fiction

Historical fiction is a favorite of some teens, but for others it is difficult to relate to. Many reluctant readers find the genre boring. These books are often too much like an assignment or lesson. Author Vivian Vande Velde explains that the title of her book *There's a Dead Person Following My Sister Around* disguises the historical lesson of the Underground Railroad, and thus more readers will give it a try (Vande Velde, 2000). In these books, if you focus on the parts about growing up that are still relevant today, you have a better chance of success with those who are not fans of historical fiction.

The American Girl, Dear America, and the American Diary series— along with their many imitators—are popular choices for some younger YA readers, especially girls. Although series in this genre are lacking for the older teen, it may be appropriate to add some non-series titles if your audience includes historical fiction fans. Diana Tixier Herald attributes the popularity of historical fiction among many teens to "the adventure and romance of dashing heroes and heroines set in different times" (Herald, 1997, p.13). Others will think of this genre as more of a history lesson than entertainment.

Science Fiction and Fantasy

Science fiction and fantasy are grouped together because they often cross over. Science fiction deals primarily with stories based on known scientific principles and possible outcomes of contemporary

> problems like pollution, population, politics, and sexual mores projected into the future for a new perspective. Fantasy creates an imagined world in which characters and events operate within established rules; no matter how imaginative, fantasy must have a convincing reality of its own in the midst of things that cannot happen to characters with superhuman powers in unreal worlds (Arnold, 1998, p. 14).

While these definitions clarify the difference, young adult or juvenile science fiction and fantasy often combine elements of both genres.

Although these genres are popular with some young adults, they will have limited appeal in a small room full of teenagers. Be sure, then, to choose books where the protagonists are hiding their shape-shifting or alien selves from their friends, where the boyfriend is the killer, or where the fantasy is acted out. True, teens who are fans of these genres are often rabid readers, eager to consume an entire set (like the *Earthsea Trilogy*, by Ursula K. Le Guin, *The Dark Is Rising*, by Susan Cooper, *Dark Materials*, by Philip Pullman, *Redwall*, by Brian Jacques, and *Everworld*, by K. A. Applegate) and the popularity of TV shows like *The X-Files* and movies like *Star Wars* provides an additional tie-in. But the teens in the audience who love these books are a minority. Others may prefer the softer books in these genres (like the *Roswell* series, by Melinda Metz, or the *Buffy the Vampire Slayer* series, or books about witches and aliens). According to some teen surveys, science fiction and fantasy do rate very high in interest and popularity. Nevertheless, reluctant readers tend not to be big fans of these genres.

Much of the science fiction and fantasy written for today's teens focuses on the present. The *Subtle Knife* starts in the present and shifts between different worlds. *The Dark Side of Nowhere* is about teens in school today who just happen to be aliens. The *Roswell* series uses aliens in a human world and at school. The variety of books available in these genres is astounding—they can include anything from wishes to morphing. The Harry Potter books by J. K. Rowling and television programs about witches have increased the popularity of these genres, even for the usual nonreaders.

Romance

Romances are as vital to some teen readers as love itself. Some teens persist in subscribing to an idealistic view of love as reflected in the pop culture. Sometimes the unpopular teen in these books gets the person of his or her dreams, which may not reflect reality. Today the genre includes books about relationships in a much broader sense than in the not-so-distant past. For example, today's romances do not always have a happy ending. Today's teens live in an increasingly complex world, and the literature about their relationships reflects that complexity. The media have made this generation of teenagers more aware of sex and sexual issues. Gay rights, abortion, sexually transmitted diseases, contemporary interpretations of moral and religious issues all are addressed in what can legitimately be called romances for YAs.

Today's teen romances are not usually the Harlequin-type books of the past. (Titles by Lurlene McDaniels, who interweaves plots involving romance and personal tragedy, thus offering books for the traditional romantics, however, are an exception.) Series tend not to be called *True Love* but instead something more modern, like *Making Out*, by Katherine Applegate. If mentioned in a booktalk, these books will most likely turn off the boys, so be careful to include some titles that might appeal to them, too. Choose books that focus on a relationship, but that aren't too sappy. Look for titles that include some other hooks, such as humor and reality in *Burger Wuss*, where a guy will do anything to get the girl and doesn't, or *Hard Love*, where a guy won't give up on his ideal woman even though she is a lesbian. Focusing on books with a male main character will help you get the boys' attention when love is the topic.

The fun thing about romances is that teens all have or want relationships, so there are plenty of chances to be funny and creative in booktalks for these titles. You can relate the embarrassing mishaps and situations that teens can identify with in their own lives; these accounts will likely appeal to the romance fans as well as the opponents.

Fairy Tales

Today's fairy tales for young adults are often either fractured or extended versions of traditional tales—that is, what the Brothers Grimm might have written if they lived today or if they had written in more detail. For example, whereas the swelling belly of Rapunzel is glanced over in a picture book, the seduction may be a major plot element in a YA or adult version (and may prompt the booktalker to consider the book's appropriateness for particular audiences). Since there are so many fairy tales, ranging from the gruesome to the sexual and romantic, it probably will be a long time before writers run out of material to turn into YA novels. These stories are so numerous that they are being requested by teen patrons, especially girls, as a genre type. Other young adults have outgrown the fairy tales they loved as a child and want no more of them.

If you think there may be an interest in these books, go ahead and use them. A quick mention is best for this genre, though, since they know the stories. Tell them that these books are different from the stories they know from childhood—maybe *very* different. Examples are *Kissing the Witch: Old Tales in New Skins,* where characters would rather kiss the women than the princes, and *The Rose and the Beast: Fairy Tales Retold,* where the females control their own fate in a world of drugs and suicide.

Short Stories

Short stories are fun because you can sum them up with a few quick sentences, or, if they are all on a similar subject, sum up the theme of the collection with a reference to one story. These books often sit on the shelves largely unread, though—perhaps because reading them does not inspire a sense of accomplishment or perhaps because it is difficult to write a report or character analysis on a collection of stories. Booktalkers can use short stories to their advantage, though, by mentioning that a teacher will never know if students skip a story or two. You know in your heart that you aren't doing any lasting damage in suggesting such subterfuge, because you know that the stories are good, and if the students have time, they really will read them all. If the stories interconnect, as in *Life Is Funny* or *Crush,* they'll have to keep reading. But it really is OK if they skip a story by an author or on a subject they don't like. Think of it as analogous to reading selected articles in a magazine or fast forwarding through scenes in a soap opera. To write booktalks for short stories, devise a list of phrases or words about what happens in each story and connect them to make an effective short story booktalk. If you prefer to focus on only one short story from a collection, make sure it fairly represents the rest of the collection.

Mystery

Mystery and adventure were in the top percentage of books of interest to boys and girls in the SmartGirl.com and Houston Public Library surveys described in Chapter 1. Mysteries do not necessarily have to be Agatha Christie or Sherlock Holmes whodunits. They need not even have the word "mystery" in the title or in the CIP data. Instead, a mere element of mystery is enough—something that someone is searching for or hiding from, a secret that is being kept from classmates or parents. Thrillers and suspense novels abound. These items will fare better with teens than the traditional mystery where murder or crime is the main plot. A book like John Marsden's *Letters from the Inside* becomes a mystery to readers who must figure out what happened to one of the young letter writers and discover where she is. The same idea evolves in *The Killer's Cousin*. Besides not knowing if David actually did kill his girlfriend, readers are unsure about the cousin, as well. There are no obvious clues in *Sang Spell*, but the truth about a town and the protagonist's escape from it must be discovered. Play up the mystery in your booktalk. Let your audience know something is to be discovered besides the plot and the ending so that they feel the same responsibility as the characters to discover the truth.

Adventure

An adventure doesn't have to involve braving death in the wilderness. It can involve a character's search or escape from someone or something with danger along the way. These books, too, can cross over into other genres. In *Teen Genreflecting* Herald identifies such titles as *Tomorrow When the War Began*, by John Marsden, and *Flash Fire*, by Caroline Cooney, as adventures (Herald, 1997, pp. 75–77). Survival is the key element here. Herald also notes that book lists on this subject are rare.

Popular adventure selections for teenagers are often found in the adult collection. Works by Tom Clancy, Clive Cussler, and John Grisham tend to be more suspenseful than the adventure novels written for children and young adults. Some of the best selections for this genre are true stories—Jon Krakauer's books are good examples along with other titles about climbing or the outdoors, such as *Within Reach: My Everest Story*. Any true adventure will do. Just as the movie *The Blair Witch Project* is scarier if you believe it is a real documentary, teens find the real adventure stories scarier or more amazing or shocking than the ones they know were invented by an author.

Nonfiction

Many students prefer to read about personal interests such as skateboarding or astrology instead of fiction. It is important to provide nonfiction books as options. The great thing about nonfiction is that it is often assigned in school. You can use this fact to your advantage by saying that you know they sometimes have to write reports on a nonfiction book, and this might be one to think about. An easy one to sell is *Who Killed My Daughter?*, by Lois Duncan, because it reads like a story. It can also segue into her book *Psychic Connections: A Journey Into the Mysterious World of Psi* in a quick mention. You are not telling them to read it now, but some may not wait for that nonfiction assignment. They will also figure out that they don't necessarily have to read the whole thing. They can skip the chapter on astral projection if it does not interest them or does not fit their purpose. Mention this approach to garner interest in any nonfiction book.

Nonfiction can be visually appealing. For those who are put off by a thick book, many nonfiction books are thinner volumes and include photographs that not only add interest and appeal but also make the reading less daunting. It is also easier to cater to current interests with paperback books on hot topics, such as movie or television tie-ins, relationships, sports, or hobbies. Take into account when presenting these popular titles, however, that a band that is popular with junior high students one day, for example, may be "out" the next. One week a TV show will be popular and the next week it will be cancelled. Try to keep topics contemporary without focusing on fads. You have to appear to know what is "in."

Short or Thin Books

Many students have found themselves in the situation where they forgot to do (or more likely put off doing) a book report until the last minute. This can be a useful context in which to tell the students about the really short books that can get them out of trouble. Let them know that it is OK to read a short book, as long as it fits the requirements of the assignment. In fact, some students may want to read, but English is not their first language or they find reading difficult. Short books, many of high quality, can be booktalked to help meet such needs.

You can say something like:

> OK, you get to school and your friend asks, "What book did you read for the book report?" You ask, "What book report?" "The one that's due today, sixth period." You say a word I can't say in this classroom, run to the library, and find [insert book's title] which is only 70 pages long. You read it in between classes, and slip it in your math book, you type your report up during lunch, and you are ready to hand it in during sixth period. Maybe not an A, but at least you're not failing the class.

Even if they don't read this book now, they'll make a note of it for later.

Don't be afraid to say, "And it is really only half as long, because every other page is a picture," for a book like *Making Up Megaboy*, or, "It appears to be 132 pages, but you only have to read 66 because half of it is in Spanish," for Gary Paulsen's *Sisters/Hermanas*. You might tell them that "*Crush* has blank pages in between the stories, so after reading only five pages you are already on page 11," or that "The pages are skinny with wide margins on the ends meaning few words to a page," in Paulsen's *The Tent: A Parable in One Sitting*. For a book of scary stories, like *When Nobody's Home: Fifteen Babysitting Tales of Terror*, you could tell them that it is OK if they don't read all the stories, since it might be too scary to finish. For books written as poetry (such as *Out of the Dust, Make Lemonade, Jump Ball: A Basketball Season in Poems*, or *Stop Pretending*) you can tell them how many fewer words are on a page since the book is in poetry form. You can even note that "There are big spaces between the characters' lines in the 88-page play *Nerdlandia* and you can skip over the stage directions, since you won't be acting out the play anyway." They will appreciate your honesty and willingness to help them out.

These tips might sound like a cruel trick to play on the teacher, but the student is asking you to identify the shortest book you have and it is your job to provide what students ask for. There are even whole books on the subject: *100 World-Class Thin Books or What to Read When Your Book Report Is Due Tomorrow!* and *The World's Best Thin Books: What to Read When Your Book Report Is Due Tomorrow*, by Joni Bodart. Bodart describes a "thin book" as one under 200 pages (Bodart, 1993, p. xiii). Most will want her "thinnest" selections. I think a short book is one around 150 pages; teenagers think it is one under 100. Consider which is better—a student selecting a short book and reading it or selecting a long book and then not finishing it or just reading the back cover? Don't worry. It is perfectly acceptable to recommend short books.

Horror

With the continuing popularity of horror films and series books, it should not be difficult to get teens to read more of these books. This genre was rated the highest in a Houston Public Library Teen Read Week and on SmartGirl.com surveys. These are the books most often requested by teenagers visiting a library, although nothing is ever scary enough for these teenagers. Take advantage of current movies and, when appropriate, draw parallels to books you are promoting.

"The plots usually involve teen-age protagonists engaged in typical American activities—attending sleep-away camp, doing volunteer work in a hospital, heading off to college—who meet with the most appalling fates" (Tucker, 1993, p. 29). This scenario is very common in horror series for young adults. Perhaps it is the hint of reality combined with the horror of the fantasy that attracts teenagers. Keep in mind that horror can also cross over into suspense or mystery. Horror can involve a variety of topics of interest to teens. There are werewolves in *Blood and*

Chocolate, a serial killer in *Tenderness*, and a killer friend in *Gorgeous*. No one book will satisfy every horror fan, so a variety is needed for this genre as well. Everyone has different fears and phobias.

Realistic Contemporary Fiction

Whether they realize it or not, most teenagers do most of their book reading in realistic contemporary fiction, and the majority of YA fiction is published in this genre. You can't go wrong here. Almost everyone enjoys a good story about someone with similar experiences. Many teens will enjoy reading about the kind of person they are or the kind of person they wish they were. We all have experienced moments when books or movies or current events inspire us. As educators, we can present books that let teenagers know they are not alone in the world, or that will give them hope for a better future. They can read about the life they want, as well as the life they have. These books often describe the kinds of relationships, problems, and situations that teenagers are going through, so in a booktalk it is not difficult to pull out a scene, come up with a question, or make up an amusing situation that they can identify with in their own lives. "The best books for young adults are the books that most truly interpret to them the process of living" (Edwards, 1994, p. 109), and thus realistic fiction has strong appeal.

Most fiction for this age group has a realistic base. Even horror series (like *Fear Street* and *Roswell*) have everyday characters. Many, if not most, young adult authors write realistic fiction, and the emerging young adult authors are also telling stories this way.

With these books, the booktalker must be sensitive to the needs of the audience. This responsibility can be problematic when booktalking about the controversial subjects common in many of the best of today's YA books. Students in the audience may relate to such subjects as divorce, a weight problem, child abuse, and eating disorders, but it may be difficult to present these subjects in a booktalk without making some people in the audience uncomfortable. Such topics as people with disabilities, the elderly, homosexuality, teen sex, drug abuse, and pregnancy present a similar challenge.

Stereotyping and harassment by their peers are very real problems faced by teens. The booktalker must be aware that students can tease their fellow classmates cruelly about such matters; in some situations, these topics may get laughs or jeers instead of interest. Contemporary realistic fiction can help teenagers sort through their problems and recognize that they are not alone or that there is hope for a solution. While some students may very well be dealing with these issues or situations, the majority of students in one room will not. You are probably not there to give a lecture on equality and tolerance, and you have most likely not been asked to provide bibliotherapy. A book like *Life in the Fat Lane* may be an excellent book for a teenager dealing with a weight problem, but if you say something like "Lara weighs 200 pounds," you have given students the opportunity to put down the "fat girl" in class. It is important to anticipate this possibility and maintain sufficient rapport with the audience to minimize the chance that this sort of thing might happen.

Monica Edinger, a fourth-grade teacher at the Dalton School in New York City read and enjoyed *Joey Pigza Loses Control*. She would have loved to read it to her class, but each year she has at least one student who resembles the main character and she does not want that student to be labeled as a "Joey" by his or her peers (Edinger, 2001). Still others choose to use this Newbery honor book because students can relate to it. A teacher or librarian must always assess the situation carefully before presenting such titles.

The issue of homosexuality is a tough call. Teens can be cruel, and although many are accepting and open-minded, others will not be. It is often best to introduce this theme with a book of short stories, or a book where the topic is not the focus of the book, but it can still be mentioned in a talk. Seventh graders tend not to handle the subject of homosexuality as a topic of a booktalk in as mature a manner as high school students. A 1997 study by the Gay Lesbian and Straight Education Network (which surveyed 496 lesbian, gay, bisexual, and transgender teenagers in 32 states) showed that 91.4 percent heard homophobic remarks from students and 36.6 percent did so from teachers. Even homosexual teachers who are supposed to be respected by their students and colleagues have similar experiences. There are academic environments where gay and lesbian student organizations or networks exist, but they are not present in most schools (Davis, 2000, p. 29).

We live in a diverse society and want our collections to meet the needs of every reader. Our booktalks, too, can reach out to those diverse readers' needs and interests. Present the best of these books, but remember to bear in mind the sophistication (or lack thereof) of your audience—sensitivity is required. It is important to make certain that the way you present the books will serve your purpose and not hurt those who appear to be different.

Humor

Most everyone likes a good laugh. Many books have their humorous moments—and some have many moments—but not many can keep everyone laughing. Just as we do not all laugh at the same jokes and just as not everyone laughs during a Jim Carrey or Adam Sandler film, not everyone will find the same YA book funny. In fact, it is rare to find a YA book that every reader will find amusing. This fact presents special problems for the booktalker who wants to present humorous books.

The books that you find funny may not be funny to your audience. Some readers may find a book funny that you thought was rather serious. Not every guy will find the humor in *Angus, Thongs and Full-Frontal Snogging: Confessions of Georgia Nicolson* or *The Girls' Guide to Hunting and Fishing*, and not every girl will think *The Education of Robert Nifkin* or *Harris and Me* is amusing. So be sure to include several different examples or styles of humorous books to appeal to the broadest possible range of potential readers. If the book is not completely funny, you can always make your booktalk humorous to get their attention.

Adult Books

Keep in mind that it is mostly the fifth through sixth graders who read the fiction we label as YA. High school students often think these titles are too young for them, especially if the books are still kept in the youth section. Many teens say they stop reading YA books after age 12 when they feel they are too old to visit the young adult sections in bookstores, according to the Bruno & Ridgeway survey (Ferguson, 1998, p. 31). Also, it is in middle school that some teens start to lose interest in reading (November, 1998, p. 775).

You want to show teens that you know they aren't interested in books for children. Similarly, you can let them know that you understand that they aren't interested in books exclusively about adult issues and concerns. There are thousands of good books published as adult titles that fall into that middle ground. Many adult books, for example, begin with a chapter on the character's youth or adolescence and lead into the character's adult life (*Offsides, World of Pies, Hundred Secret Senses, Local Girls, It*, and *The Girls' Guide to Hunting and Fishing*). Teenagers can perhaps relate to parts of the stories and then speculate as they read about what is in store for them compared to the fictional world created by the author.

When speaking in high schools especially, try to have at least half of your booktalk titles be ones published for an adult audience. Ninth through twelfth graders can read and enjoy the best of YA titles with older protagonists and sophisticated plots, but they tend to want to read more adult titles, too. It is important to provide booktalks about the best new books available from the world of adult publishing when addressing the high school audience. This need to include adult titles is great for you, too—it gives you the perfect excuse to take a break and read a book for yourself every once and awhile.

Appropriate adult books are easy to find, since professional review journals often highlight such titles. *VOYA* gives a rating of A/YA for adult-marketed books recommended for YAs, *School Library Journal* has a section of "Adult Books for Young Adults," and *Booklist* identifies YA books in the adult books section by adding a bold YA after each review with a note of why it is appropriate for young adults. Each year since 1998 YALSA's "Adult Books for Young Adults Task Force" has selected ten outstanding titles published for adults that should have wide appeal to older teens for the Alex Award (*www.ala.org/yalsa/awards/ alextxt.html*). The 1990s brought about an increased awareness and publishing of young adult literature, but the 21st century trend seems to be to market books for adults with younger high school or college or twenty-something characters. There is also more sexual content in adult books, which tends to interest older teenagers.

Teen magazines and Web sites now often review adult books. Again, you must be aware of the possibility of mature content if you use these titles with younger YAs. Selecting librarians must keep in mind their YA customers, as well as the community and the collection development policies of the library. If a book's sexual content goes significantly beyond one's "normal" YA or PG-13 comfort level, a public library might shelve it in the adult section, so it can still be promoted at the high school but to lessen the chance that the fourth and fifth graders who sometimes delve into the YA collection will stumble on it.

If you are a school librarian, you may have even stricter guidelines governing selection. Coordinate with your local public librarian so that teens know they are not limited to the school's collection. In many communities interlibrary loan can significantly improve the selection available to teen customers. Take advantage of such opportunities when booktalking to publicize such services so that more adult books and a variety of others are made available to all young adults.

Graphic Novels

Graphic novels (novels that look similar to comic books) don't necessarily have to be the Superman-type comic books of the past. They now include such additions as *The Freddie Stories*, *The Amazing True Story of a Teenage Single Mom*, and *Pedro and Me: Friendship, Loss, and What I Learned*. Books like these can provide a hook, and then even reluctant teen readers may ask what else you have. After all, the books can be over 200 pages long—they just don't have many words, so they can foster a sense of accomplishment and they make reading a little easier on the eyes. A book report doesn't have to mention the pictures. If you have graphic novels or comic books, you might want to mention which series you own, even if you don't booktalk them. If you are clueless about where to begin, try Kat Kan's "Graphically Speaking" column in *VOYA* for suggestions.

Poetry

In this age of poetry slams and coffeehouses, it is worth reflecting on the fact that poetry remains one of the most important types of litera- ture for many teens, not so much because they love to read it, but be- cause they love to write it. Such has long been the case. According to Carlsen, "The average reader reads much less poetry than prose in a life- time, but poetry is still of great importance" (Carlsen, 1980, p. 170). He says that teens claim to prefer humorous poems, but they choose epics or classics as their favorites. Interest in poetry is often dependent on the teacher and the education a student receives. Poetry is sometimes over- analyzed, making students uninterested in reading it for fun. Thankfully, some learn to read poetry as a mystery and discover its beauty, appreci- ate its power, and enjoy reading it as well as writing it as a means of self-expression.

Although many students do attend poetry slams and write and pub- lish their own poetry, it is not often a favorite with reluctant readers. If these teens have to read poems, they prefer Shel Silverstein to Percy Bysshe Shelley. They are more likely to be interested in Edgar Allan Poe's poetry or in recent teen poetry collections (such as *The Pain Tree and Other Teenage Angst-Ridden Poetry*) than the poems of Emily Dickinson or other classical poets of western literature.

There will always be teens who never get it, and not only will they not enjoy poetry, but they will have no sense of accomplishment from reading a book of poems they do not understand. There is no reason to expect everyone to love this genre. Just make them aware of some po- etry they might enjoy, and don't worry if the 811s stay on the shelves.

SPECIAL SITUATIONS EVERY BOOKTALKER ENCOUNTERS

What to Do When You Hate the Book

Sometimes even you—a librarian or a teacher—will dislike a well-re- viewed book, but it happens. Try to assess your personal prejudices and think about the reasons for your negative responses. Don't worry if you did not like a book. Just like any other reader, you are entitled to personal tastes and preferences. Any reader will disagree with reviews on occasion. The reader may laugh throughout *Truth or Dairy* and later read the *Kirkus* review stating that it was only "faintly amusing" and "straining for laughs." It is critically important to remember that a review is the opinion of one individual reader/writer. The reviewer is human, too, and is largely expressing a personal response to the book. If all readers/reviewers had the same tastes, there would be no need for more than one review of each book. Even Newbery award winners sometimes receive mixed reviews.

If you dislike a book, that does not mean you should keep the book from others. What about a book that isn't great writing, but you know the students will like it? These books may just bring teens to the YA section—where they will find other books they like, and where you have slipped in some great YA books, some adult titles, and maybe even some classics with updated covers. What if you do not like a book for another reason? Maybe it just did not interest you. Most booktalkers agree that you should not talk about a book you did not like. Some may even say that you have to love the book in order to make others love it too. But if you just talk about books you love, then the students may never have the opportunity to hear about the books they could love. They may just be looking for the book that you put down. Be open-minded in your selection.

Getting the Right Books to the Right Readers at the Right Time

If you booktalk at a parochial school or are considering it, be mindful to respect their beliefs. You are a guest, so make sure you do not use books that might obviously offend (for example, books with a lot of sex, those with excessive violence, or those that are overly explicit about the use of illegal drugs). This rule also holds true for many conservative junior high schools or elementary schools where all age levels attend.

The majority of my booktalks are for students in seventh through tenth grade. Most of the younger YAs are still reading and getting support from their classroom teacher, and I seldom get the opportunity to booktalk to the older high school students. So when I was asked to add talks to the sixth-grade classrooms on the same day I was to visit only seventh and eighth graders, I quickly had to change the books on my list. Later, I walked into a room and discovered to my surprise that a class of seventh and eighth graders was all boys who were at a lower reading level. I quickly made further changes, removing the "girl" books from the batch, adding some that I would use with sixth grade.

Try to know as much as you can about your audience. If possible and if there is time, talk in advance to the teacher or principal so you are both on the same page concerning the audience, purpose, time frame, and other expectations. Most sixth graders are into "boys" or "girls" and they see violence on TV, movies, and video games. They know that evil things go on in the world, but they generally have limited experiences. They are still a little bit too far from a car or the prom to care about these subjects, and many have not yet reached puberty. In these situations I often cut out much of the sexual hinting I would use in a high school classroom and in some junior highs. (See the section "Lie a Little" in Chapter 3.) At least in the upper grades, I know they are reading books like *The Scarlet Letter* and not *Sounder*.

Too Many Teens, Too Few Books

Ideally, you should have multiple copies of books for the mad rush of students after your talk. But in reality, some libraries, especially school media centers, cannot afford this. Current titles may not always be available in paperback. You may prefer to spend your budget on needed materials to support the curriculum rather than on multiple copies of fiction titles. Or you may choose to add extra copies once you are certain a title is popular rather than anticipating what will be popular.

Your collection should ideally have at least one paperback copy of a title if that format is available, since many teens prefer to read paperbacks. You might want to purchase your own copy of the books you use most often so the library copy can circulate even while you present booktalks. You might also consider using interlibrary loan to get copies for booktalks, again so your library's copy is available for circulation while it is fresh in the students' minds. Librarians and teachers can check books out from the library in the community in which they reside for the same purpose. Then you can leave bookmarks out in your library featuring titles you talked, along with the books and a sign reading something like "Books as featured at Reavis High School." That may even entice younger readers who usually enjoy reading books about older characters.

Another option is to present a variety of talks for different classrooms, grades, or schools to spread out the demand for individual titles. This is ideal, but the obvious problem with this approach is that it takes more time to read enough YA books and to write, memorize, learn, or practice enough booktalks for several different sessions or schools. Eventually, you will be able to do this, but don't worry if you cannot at first. There is the chance that you will repeat booktalks to the same students from one year to the next, so keep a record of what you use. After gaining experience for a year or two you will begin to have a solid enough repertoire that you won't duplicate talks to a seventh grader who has moved up to eighth grade.

On the other hand, you might also prefer to use your best talks every time. The quality of the talks is more important than having the books available immediately. Most students are willing to put their names on a waiting list, and most students are willing to find another book in the meantime.

Choosing Books for Diverse Groups

Vary the types of books to accommodate as wide a range as possible of reading difficulty, interest, ethnicity, culture, genre, and so on, unless you have a specific reason to do otherwise (such as a request to present books only of a particular type).

THE GIRLS AND THE BOYS

Balance the books you select between those that might appeal mostly to girls and those specifically aimed at boys, although those that appeal to both are the best choice. There is a growing new trend to publish books with "girls" in the title. The resurgence of the "girl power" movement has helped this trend along. Titles include *Girls on Film, Girls on the Verge, Girls Know Best: Advice for Girls from Girls on Just About Everything,* and *The Real Rules for Girls.*

It is interesting that for many years a book title like *Basketball for Girls* or even *Basketball for Boys* was acceptable. Then that became politically incorrect. The Sunlink Weed of the Month Club (*www.sunlink.ucf.edu/weed*) and other weeding sources suggest removing such titles from a collection. Now we are back to giving "girls" their own identities and an independent voice. If they are never going to be in the NBA, then it is OK for them to have the WNBA. It is OK for girls to achieve in a sport of their own rather than be mixed in with the boys and never have the hope of a professional career. Also, it is OK for them to want books on beauty and relationships.

Girls are not alone. More books are also available with "boys" or "guys" in the title, on subjects other than sports, including *The Teenage Guy's Survival Guide, Boys Know It All: Wise Thoughts and Wacky Ideas from Guys Just Like You,* and *From Boys to Men: All About Adolescence and You.*

It is important not to focus too much on those titles that will only appeal to one gender. If you work in a school and often present new books to the classes, it may be routine to show and talk about a variety of new books. But if you have limited time and if, for example, you are in a school only once a year, you might rather choose books that will possibly appeal to both genders (rather than limiting appeal with titles words like "girl" or "boy").

MULTICULTURAL

It is critical in today's increasingly diverse culture that booktalkers include at least a fair sampling of multicultural books. Nowhere is the need for such books greater than in communities that lack cultural and ethnic diversity. You do not want to exclude anyone and you cannot always anticipate who will be in the audience or what their tastes will be. For example, a teacher at an all-white Catholic grade school in the Chicago area told me that her seventh and eighth graders' favorite author is Gary Soto. One never knows.

STEREOTYPES

Think of the variety of teens represented in most schools and communities. They may include kids who are called (or call themselves) nerds, gang bangers, jocks, brains, geeks, freaks, punks, ravers, hip-hoppers, break dancers, brains, preps, Goths, bandies, hippies, metal heads, pretty girls, pretty boys, druggies, Abercrombies, band geeks, and skaters. You can probably fill in some more terms from your own neighborhood. These labels and others like them are coined because they represent real kids who need to belong, to identify with friends, and find their own place in the world. Kids are labeled because they are in theatre, because they look or act like someone else, or because they listen to a certain type of music or prefer art and literature to video games and parties. Whatever they are called, there are more cliques than there used to be, thus reflecting our more diverse culture. There are so many more ways now for students to show individuality, yet still be part of a group.

Many good books feature these types of teenagers. The protagonists are going through the same experiences as the teens we meet every day. They ask the same questions. Should I have sex? Does so and so like me? What will I do when I graduate? They feel the same pain when they are rejected by a person or a college, fail a test, or get caught or grounded. They feel the same disappointment when they are not invited to a dance or when their feelings for another person are not reciprocated, or the same excitement when their crush finally responds to them. Yet they all look and act differently. Books like *Slave Day* and *Life Is Funny* interweave the lives of what can be seen as a variety of stereotypical characters. They illuminate the lives of real teens facing tough choices. Offering books for a variety of types of students is just as important as offering a variety of genres and cultures. Mix them up and offer options to appeal to as many people as possible.

REFERENCES

Arnold, Mary. 1998. "'I Want Another Book Like…': Young Adults and Genre Literature." In *Young Adults and Public Libraries: A Handbook of Materials and Services*. Westport, Conn.: Greenwood Press.

Bodart, Joni. 1992. *100 World-Class Thin Books or What to Read When Your Book Report Is Due Tomorrow!* Englewood, Colo.: Libraries Unlimited.

Bodart, Joni. 2000. *The World's Best Thin Books: What to Read When Your Book Report Is Due Tomorrow.* Lanham, Md.: Scarecrow Press.

Carlsen, G. Robert. 1980. *Books and the Teenage Reader: A Guide for Teachers, Librarians and Parents.* New York: Harper & Row.

Cheskin Research. *Teens and the Future of the Internet.* *www.cheskin.com/think/studies/netteens.html* (August, 1999).

Davis, Gode. 2000. *Joey Magazine* 3 (Fall): 26–30.

Edinger, Monica R. "Joey Pigza," CCBC-Net. *www.soemadison.wisc.edu/ccbc/listserv.htm* (January 30, 2001).

Edwards, Margaret. 1994. *The Fair Garden and the Swarm of Beasts: The Library and the Young Adult.* Chicago: American Library Association.

Ferguson, Amanda. 1998. "Reading Seen as Cool." *Publishers Weekly* 245 (October 12): 28–31.

Harvey, Mary. 2000. "Let's Hear It for the Boys." *American Demographics* 22 (August): 30–33.

Herald, Diana Tixier. 1997. *Teen Genreflecting*. Englewood, Colo.: Libraries Unlimited.

November, Sharyn. 1998. "Field Notes: I'm Not a Teenage—I Just Read Like One." *Horn Book* 74 (November/December): 775.

Rochman, Hazel. 1987. *Tales of Love and Terror: Booktalking the Classics, Old and New.* Chicago: American Library Association.

Tucker, Ken. 1993. "Nameless Fear Stalks the Middle-Class Teen-Ager: Perhaps It Is the Fear of Boredom." *New York Times Book Review* 143 (November 14): 27–29.

Vande Velde, Vivian. September 29, 2000. Speaker at Northern Illinois Young Adult Literature Conference. College of DuPage, Glen Ellyn, Ill.

BOOKS FOR TEENS MENTIONED IN THIS CHAPTER

Anderson, Matthew T. 1999. *Burger Wuss*. Cambridge, Mass.: Candlewick Press.

Armstrong, William Howard. 1969. *Sounder*. New York: Harper & Row.

Arnoldi, Katherine. 1998. *The Amazing True Story of a Teenage Single Mom*. New York: Hyperion.

Banks, Melissa. 1999. *The Girls' Guide to Hunting and Fishing*. New York: Viking Press.

Barry, Lynda. 1999. *The Freddie Stories*. Seattle: Sasquatch Books.

Bates, Michael. 1995. *Gorgeous*. New York: Bantam.

Bennett, Cherie. 1998. *Life in the Fat Lane*. New York: Delacorte Press.

Blais, Madeleine. 1995. *In These Girls Hope Is a Muscle*. New York: Warner Books.

Block, Francesca Lia. 2000. *The Rose and the Beast: Fairy Tales Retold*. New York: HarperCollins.

Bronte, Emily. 1847. *Wuthering Heights*. Hauppauge, N.Y.: Barron's.

Bundy, Clare, Lise Carrigg, Sibyl Goldman, and Andrea Pyros. 1999. *Girls on Film*. New York: HarperPerennial.

Clark, Catherine. 2000. *Truth or Dairy*. New York: HarperTempest.

Conford, Ellen. 1998. *Crush*. New York: HarperCollins.

Cooney, Caroline. 1995. *Flash Fire*. New York: Scholastic.

Cormier, Robert. 1997. *Tenderness*. New York: Delacorte Press.

Daldry, Jeremy. 1999. *The Teenage Guy's Survival Guide*. Boston: Little, Brown.

Deuker, Carl. 1997. *Painting the Black*. Boston: Houghton Mifflin.

Donoghue, Emma. 1997. *Kissing the Witch: Old Tales in New Skins*. New York: HarperCollins.

Duncan, Lois. 1992. *Who Killed My Daughter?* New York: Delacorte Press.

Duncan, Lois. 1995. *Psychic Connections: A Journey into the Mysterious World of Psi*. New York: Delacorte Press.

Frank, E. R. 2000. *Life Is Funny*. New York: DK.

Glenn, Mel. 1997. *Jump Ball: A Basketball Season in Poems*. New York: Lodestar Books.

Gorog, Judith. 1996. *When Nobody's Home: Fifteen Babysitting Tales of Terror*. New York: Scholastic.

Gurian, Michael. 1999. *From Boys to Men: All About Adolescence and You*. New York: Price Stern Sloan.

Hawthorne, Nathaniel. 1850. *The Scarlet Letter*. Boston: Ticknor and

Fields.

Hesse, Karen. 1997. *Out of the Dust*. New York: Scholastic.

Hoffman, Alice. 1999. *Local Girls*. New York: G. P. Putnam's Sons.

King, Stephen. 1986. *It*. New York: Viking Press.

Klause, Annette Curtis. 1997. *Blood and Chocolate*. New York: Delacorte Press.

Lee, Marie G. 1996. *Necessary Roughness*. New York: HarperCollins.

Littman, Jonathan. 1999. *The Beautiful Game: Sixteen Girls and the Soccer Season That Changed Everything*. New York: Avon Books.

Madden-Lunsford, Kerry. 1996. *Offsides*. New York: William Morrow.

Marsden, John. 1994. *Letters from the Inside*. Boston: Houghton Mifflin.

Marsden, John. 1995. *Tomorrow When the War Began*. Boston: Houghton Mifflin.

Melville, Herman. 1851. *Moby Dick*. New York: Bantam Books.

Morgenstern, Minday. 2000. *The Real Rules for Girls*. Los Angeles: Girl Press.

Naylor, Phyllis Reynolds. 1998. *Sang Spell*. New York: Atheneum Books for Young Readers.

The Pain Tree and Other Teenage Angst-Ridden Poetry. 2000. Boston: Houghton Mifflin.

Paulsen, Gary. 1993. *Harris and Me: A Summer Remembered*. San Diego: Harcourt Brace.

Paulsen, Gary. 1993. *Sisters/Hermanas*. San Diego: Harcourt Brace.

Paulsen, Gary. 1995. *The Tent: A Parable in One Sitting*. San Diego: Harcourt Brace.

Pfetzer, Mark. 1998. *Within Reach: My Everest Story*. New York: Dutton Books.

Pinkwater, Daniel. 1998. *The Education of Robert Nifkin*. New York: Farrar, Straus & Giroux.

Pullman, Philip. 1997. *A Subtle Knife*. New York: Knopf.

Rennison, Louise. 2000. *Angus, Thongs and Full-Frontal Snogging: Confessions of Georgia Nicolson*. New York: HarperCollins.

Revoyr, Nina. 1997. *The Necessary Hunger: A Novel*. New York: Simon & Schuster.

Roehm, Michelle, ed. 1997. *Girls Know Best: Advice for Girls from Girls on Just About Everything*. Milwaukee, Wisc.: Gareth Stevens.

Roehm, Michelle, ed. 1998. *Boys Know It All: Wise Thoughts and Wacky Ideas from Guys Like You*. Hillsboro, Ore.: Beyond Words.

Shusterman, Neal. 1997. *The Dark Side of Nowhere*. Boston: Little, Brown.

Sones, Sonya. 1999. *Stop Pretending: What Happened When My Big Sister Went Crazy*. New York: HarperCollins.

Soto, Gary. 1999. *Nerdlandia: A Play*. New York: PaperStar.

Stoltz, Karen. 2000. *World of Pies*. New York: Hyperion.

Tan, Amy. 1995. *Hundred Secret Senses*. New York: G. P. Putnam's Sons.

Thomas, Rob. 1997. *Slave Day*. New York: Simon & Schuster Books for Young Readers.

Vande Velde, Vivian. 1999. *There's a Dead Person Following My Sister Around*. San Diego: Harcourt Brace.

Vendala, Vida. 1999. *Girls on the Verge: Debutante Dips, Gang Drive-Bys, and Other Initiations*. New York: St. Martin's Press.

Walter, Virginia. 1998. *Making Up Megaboy*. New York: DK.

Werlin, Nancy. 1998. *The Killer's Cousin*. New York: Delacorte Press.

Wilder, Rae. 2000. *Soccer Girls*. Lincoln, NE: iUniverse.com.

Winnick, Judd. 2000. *Pedro and Me: Friendship, Loss, and What I Learned*. New York: Henry Holt.

Wittlinger, Ellen. 1999. *Hard Love*. New York: Simon & Schuster Books for Young Readers.

Wolff, Virginia Euwer. 1993. *Make Lemonade*. New York: Henry Holt.

Chapter 3

Techniques

CHOOSING YOUR DELIVERY STYLE

Relax. Don't just stand up there reading from note cards. If you have to use notes, try to reduce them to short notes for the back of the book or inside the cover. Just glance at them to recall the characters' names or ages, or the key words you need to get started talking. Strive to sound as if you are talking off the top of your head, even if you are not. This effect will happen naturally with practice.

If you are showing the cover of the book or illustrations, talk while you do so to keep the interest of those in the class who cannot see the book. You also need to walk around and move your body. This may sound silly, but you have to put it in context. When I use the book *Sirena* in a high school, and say "In order to become immortal the women must 'get together' with mortal men" (Bromann, 1999, p. 63), I bounce my hip a couple times with an inconspicuous wink on the phrase "get together" so the older crowd gets my meaning. Practice your style until you can pull it off naturally. This particular example may be a stretch for many male librarians, but they should feel free to use their own style and body language to communicate during booktalks in ways that fit them best.

Begin with confidence. Don't let their looks of disdain scare or distract you. Be aware of the guy who pretends to sharpen his pencil and sneaks up behind you to give you bunny ears or whatever they do when we're not looking. You know that if one student everyone thinks is "cool" makes a rude comment or refuses to laugh, everyone else will follow. So start off with something you are sure about.

Follow their lead. If you bring up something you think they will like, only to find out they don't, make a face of disgust, shake your head, and cover up by saying something like "Well it's nothing like what happened here." For example, I once used the movie *Drive Me Crazy* as the preface to the book it was based on, *Girl Gives Birth to Own Prom Date*. In the first class I made the mistake of saying that the girl who played "Sabrina the Teenage Witch" on TV was in the movie. Few students admitted seeing the movie. I guess "Sabrina" is not a cool show to watch, since in another class when I asked who had seen the movie (without mentioning "Sabrina"), most hands were raised and they were fine with it. Anyway, to cover in the first class, I made that "Isn't that lame?" look by scrunching up my face, shook my head, and said, "Well, this isn't like the movie" in a snotty voice.

Think twice before bringing in a cart full of books. If you push a cart in, you are automatically labeled as the librarian and the stereotype forms in their mind. Carry the books in a box or in your hands. Better yet, bring them in an Abercrombie & Fitch™ bag. Teens shop at this store, and the bag is covered with pictures of hot-looking models. I always get comments on these bags. A bag from any popular teen clothing store will probably get you that fashionable teen vote—it shows them that either you or your children shop at these stores. It's just another way to relate.

Disruptions: The Success Indicator

Let the students speak. If they have comments or questions, even to each other, that just means they are actually listening and have something to say to their friends about the books you used or about what you said. Kids talking out loud to each other during booktalks is your greatest compliment. It shows they are paying attention and that something clicked with them that they want to share with a friend. Maybe they are just saying "I read that one," or "That happened to me." So let them talk. You will be able to determine whether it is related to your talks or if it gets excessive. If it goes on too long you can wave your arms and nod in agreement until it calms down a little and they follow along again.

Teens rarely ask questions, but if they do ask, answer them. If it is not a serious question, just smile, look at them with amused disgust, give a short coughing laugh, crinkle your nose and eyes, and move on. Maybe ignore them until you finish your thought, but don't tell them to wait until the end of your presentation. They will forget or not care. Most questions can be answered with "Read the book," or "I'm not telling," spoken in a secretive, snotty tone—as they would say if they had a secret. Keep the talk moving forward, and keep control of the situation.

Keeping Them Awake

Involving the students is the most important part of keeping them focused. It also happens to be the most fun way to conduct a booktalk. If they have to think, then they are listening. If you can get them to think about something they know and that doesn't take too much effort, they are likely to answer. If you make them laugh, then they will keep listening so they can laugh some more. Tease them. Joke around with them. By using them as examples, they feel part of the action. For the book *Gallows Hill*, I start off by asking for a volunteer who wants me to try to read his or her mind. I try to pick one of the jokesters of the group, and tell him something like "I see that you hate reading. That you can't wait for school to get out. And oh, I see a girl." Then I describe a girl who is similar in looks to several of the girls in class so there can be speculation on who it is. If you choose the right student, there won't be any embarrassment, but they will laugh for the fun of it. Once I said something like "Maybe the girl is a cousin." Everyone "oohed" like I meant incest. So I tried to cover it with "Maybe he's just seeing her this weekend." But the word "seeing" took on the meaning of dating and more laughs occurred. They liked that teasing. Of course, once I picked the wrong girl who wouldn't play along. Still, I refer to her as the fortune girl whenever she comes in the library and she smiles. I then end the fortune talk with "Well, I'm not really very good at this yet. I just read a book on it." When I used this technique with adults, I accidentally guessed the truth about the volunteer. I had to skip the "I'm not very good at this yet" part and pretend I was amazed at my skill since I had only read a book on it, just as Sarah, the protagonist, was amazed at her talent in the book. No matter what the situation, I follow up with the story of how Sarah is asked to be the fortune teller at a carnival, only to discover that she really can see what is going on in her classmates' lives. The playful, interactive fortune-telling introduction to this book sets the stage for that very brief booktalk.

There is a difference between "cool" and "hurtful" teasing, however. It is funny and acceptable to be teased about boy/girl issues, but not about not having a boyfriend or girlfriend. It is funny to tease about doing something nerdy, but not about someone who is too short or overweight or who has a birthmark on her face. It is the things that can't easily be changed that cause individual teen pain. Such issues require care when addressed in booktalks.

In my booktalk for *Like Water for Chocolate*, I have said in reference to one character that "Not all men are that smart." It was meant to be a snappy, humorous put-down that anyone in the audience could relate to. Rob Reid, a librarian and university instructor from Wisconsin, wrote to me after seeing this talk in my article "The Toughest Audience on Earth" (Bromann, 1999, p. 62) to suggest that I leave that part out; he proposed that it is not necessary, and makes it seem OK to put men down (Reid, 1999). Try to be sensitive to the group you are speaking to. If, for a particular audience or situation you think it will help more or be more entertaining than hurtful, then you have to make that choice.

CHOOSING YOUR WORDS

What to Say

Pay attention to the style as well as the substance of what you say. It is so important not to allow your talk to sound like a list of books to read; instead it should sound like a conversation or announcements of what is going on in the news world of teenagers, like gossip, music videos, or movie trailers. Your talks need to be fast and to the point or you'll lose their attention. Use short, quick sentences, with short pauses to give them time to think, but keep things moving. You don't want books to sound like books. As unconventional as it may sound, to be effective in reaching out to reluctant teen readers, this is one of the most important things for a librarian/teacher to remember.

Be informal. Make it sound as if you don't care whether they read. To open, you might say something like "I know you don't have much time to read with all the homework and sports and activities and jobs you have, but I just wanted to tell you about some books you might want to read when you have to do a book report or when you're taking a long flight and need something to do." If they perceive that you are not there to *make* them read, they will be more likely to listen to you as entertainment rather than education. They might not shut you out.

Or you might start like this:

> I came today from the library to tell you about some books. Don't worry; I know you don't have any time to read. I've seen what y'all do. You go to school until three, then have a club meeting, sports, band practice, or work until maybe five or six, you eat and maybe around seven call a friend or e-mail or get online doing whatever you do, then maybe around eight you watch TV until ten because those Nielsen people who monitor your TV behavior say that teens watch an average of two hours a night, so then you can start your homework and finish around one. OK, so if you have to get up at six to do it all over again, and it takes you an hour to fall asleep because there is so much to think about and worry about what you didn't get done, and what you'll wear the next day, and if Kevin is still dating Sue, and how you can see him in between every class, or

how you're going to get out of faking a hall pass, then you have maybe four hours of sleep a night. True, you may choose to read the newest 1,000-page Stephen King novel in one sitting, but most likely you are going to try and get as much sleep as you can. So I'm not expecting you to actually read these books. I'm just going to tell you about some you might want to read if you have a book report due; if they make you read books in homeroom, study hall, or English; or if you ever have to go on a long plane flight and you finish your two magazines before the plane even takes off because your dad makes you get to the airport two hours early.

This example may seem to dismiss reading, but remember teenagers are often likely to do what they are told not to do. It is human nature and they will respect you more if you show them that you know where they are coming from. They will appreciate that you are doing them a favor by telling them about books that they might like and that will get them out of trouble and not make them have to do too much more work. They will listen to you if they know you are not necessarily there to make them read.

I use a similar tactic when I visit the classrooms to get volunteers for our summer reading program. I say something like "I'm here to tell you about our summer reading program. I know you're too old for this, but I want to ask for your help." I go on to mention that volunteering can get them good work experience so they don't have to hand in a blank job or college application. I do, of course, tell them that they can read, too, and tell them about the prizes like it's no big deal, nodding and shaking my head like I know they're not interested, yet knowing some are. I know I'm not going to win over any new readers on these days, but if they plan on volunteering I let them know the reading part is there. Then I get them to join by telling them they will help me reach my goal of 650 kids or that they probably read some teen magazines anyway, when they come to volunteer.

Although it is over 50 years old, *An Ample Field: Books and Young People*, by Amelia Munson, provides a lot of great ideas. In describing a booktalk Munson states, "At its best, it sounds informal and spontaneous and in such harmony with the group addressed that it seems like conversation or discussion rather than a monologue" (Munson, 1950, p. 99). In other words, teens should feel like you are talking to them and not giving a speech or presentation about a book. It should sound as if they are listening to a friend tell them about a book they might want to read rather than a librarian telling them about a book they should read.

How you say it is extremely important. I speak in sarcastic, playful, contemporary, and understanding tones. This helps me sound more like a peer than an authority. This may not be the tone you should use, however. How do you talk with your friends? How would you talk if you were a teenager today? How do your students or your patrons or your children talk? Be yourself. Don't go overboard, but it is most important that you present yourself as comfortable, relaxed, and ready to converse with your audience.

What Not to Say

You must also be careful of what not to say. Try not to say "Reading can be fun," or even "This is a great book," or "Here are some interesting books." Avoid saying, "I read this book," although it is so tempting. Brian Wilson, a children's librarian at Oak Lawn (Illinois) Public Library, suggests instead to tell them something like "Everyone is checking it out" (Wilson, 2000). If they question why it is on the shelf if it is so popular, point out how many times the book has been checked out, or maybe just tell them they're lucky that it is finally in. Some people believe that an audience won't trust you unless they know you read the book, but teens usually won't want to read books you like. Of course, some students will want and trust your opinion, but those who don't like reading would rather choose a novel that people their age like. So hide the fact that you read a book or just don't mention it at all. Also, try not to tell them something is cool. Let them figure that out themselves. They want and need to decide what is cool on their own. Empower them by keeping your opinions to yourself.

Avoid popular catch phrases like, "If you want to find out what happens next, read . . .," or "This is what happens in . . ." End with something like "Maybe this happens, or maybe this happens," or just end with your last thought and move on to the next book—no conclusion is necessary. If what you say interests them, they will read it anyway.

Teenagers tend to do what they're told not to do. They know you are telling them about books—you are holding a book in your hand, you are leaving them a bookmark, they see you in the library. Put down the book after you mention the title and leave it at that.

What's in a Name?

Watch what you call teenagers. This is a tough one, though, since acceptable terms may vary from one school to another, or even from one classroom to another. Be careful how you use "boy" and "girl" for example. "Guy" is usually the best choice for males, although there is no exact equivalent term for females. "Gal" will not work with this age group, and girls still don't quite feel like women at this age. "Girls" is often used by men and women alike to refer to females of any age, but males over the age of 16 are seldom called "boys," unless in a playful or derogatory way. Some studies report different findings than reality might prove. Once when I referred to the females in a seventh-grade class as "women," I got in trouble. A girl kept correcting me and said "We're girls." I wanted to tell her that as long as she had her period she was a woman. Later I looked in *The Random House College Dictionary* (1980) to find the correct definition of a woman so I would no longer be misguided. Besides the obvious definition of "the female human being," a woman is also "a female person who cleans house, cooks, etc." I'm sure this girl has cleaned and cooked before. A woman, according to this dictionary also has "feminine nature, characteristics or feeling," which means technically all the guys in the room could be women, too. How wrong was she? But to avoid the argument, I now only use "girls" and sometimes "women" in a high school. When you refer to a character in a book, "teenager" implies that you are referring to someone young. "This guy" or "this girl" are good choices, or you can use "students" in a phrase like "the students from Robert E. Lee High." After the character is introduced you can then refer to him or her by name.

This is what *I* have experienced. Your teenagers might want to be called something else. Ask around. Take a poll. Ask your advisory board. Learn with experience. If you are still not sure, vary your words until you know what they like to be called, or stick with the terms you know are safe.

You and I

Unless you are a closet thespian, avoid telling the story in the first person—the teens might picture you as the character, and a high school student or even a seventh or eighth grader will not want to read a book about you. They will read a book about themselves, though, and an excellent way to present a booktalk is by using the second person and placing the focus on the students with the word "you." They are more likely to pay attention if you talk about them rather than someone they don't know.

Remember that first-person quotes spoken on their own without introduction can be confusing. Teens may not know who is saying what. They won't know if you are talking about someone from the book or yourself or someone else. If you choose to quote in the first person, make sure your audience is aware of what you are doing. Brian Wilson uses the first person in his booktalk for *Killing Mr. Griffin.* He is a very animated person and can pull off this technique. So it is possible, especially if the students see you almost as an actor performing miniplays for them, however, it will not work well without an introduction or if it is read straight from the book.

Remember to hold back on sharing your personal experiences (unless Justin from the band 'N Sync was your neighbor, or something like that). Most students really don't care what happened to you when you were a teenager—that was, after all, somewhere in the dark ages. Personal stories can work occasionally and in small doses, especially if you already have a good relationship with your students, but if most of the students don't know you, keep them to a minimum. The focus should be on the books, not on the booktalker.

It is true, however, that many people, teens included, like to talk about themselves. You might be able to put the focus back on the teens by letting them tell some of their own stories. Alternatively, tell your story if it is something they can relate to and if it will help them remember or relate to the book—but tell it as if it happened to your son or a teenager you know. That way they can imagine the teen it happened to rather than have to picture you as a teen.

LIE A LITTLE

Hinting and lying can also liven up your talk. I am not suggesting you tell the students that a book is about sex when it is about a boy and his dog. But the mere mention of one of their favorite topics, sex, can perk up their ears and maybe make them more interested in what you are saying. That interest could lead them to the book. Let's face it, although there are different statistics, many, many teenagers in the United States are or become sexually active in their teens. If they are not having sex, they are thinking about it or are at least curious about it. Well-written, accurate, informative, engaging books that teenagers will want to read often include at least some sexual content. That interest is a normal, natural, and important part of growing up. The question of whether one should be sexually active (as our culture's advertising seems to promote almost universally) or be chaste (as our mores tend to dictate) is an important one.

Some of these books will make them happy to be virgins, encourage them to be more careful so they don't end up in the same bad situation, or help them to make their own decisions. Hinting at teenagers' favorite subjects will often get their attention. Stretching the truth a little when these topics are present, but perhaps not explicit, in a novel will bring young adults to these books. I am not suggesting you use books with explicit sex scenes, or even that you should mention the word sex. Just hint a little. They'll get it.

There is a perfect opportunity to hint with *Thumbsucker*. In this novel, Justin is hypnotized into ending his thumb-sucking habit in his teens. So I honestly say "He needed to find other ways to satisfy his oral fixation." I can't help it if sexual thoughts then enter these teenagers' minds. I tell the truth, yet my tone may indicate that it might have something to do with sex. There is a brief scene where a girl does the main character a sexual favor. I guess I could use that, too, to get their attention, but I am trying to hint and lie here, not tell the truth. For *Slave Day* after describing the characters, I say "One of them gets a little lucky." One does get lucky—he gets paired with the woman of his dreams. Again, I can't help it if they think I mean something else

Of course, out of fear of losing our jobs, we must also be aware of how much sex is in a book. Many schools have strict guidelines concerning collection development. Having the book on the shelves of a public library is one thing, but recommending it to young teen readers is another. It has been stated, "If these books were movies, many would be rated R for content and for the sprinkling of obscenities" (Morris and Eaton, 1999, p. 66). In fact, most YA books are PG-13 material, and increasingly more R material is appearing in the literature.

Lots of kids out there have high self-worth and self-discipline, have had positive role models, and possess a strong moral sense. They are mature, have long-term goals, and are ready to read about mature topics and themes that will challenge them intellectually and emotionally. Some of these teens, however, and others (especially those raised in certain religious environments) may be offended by explicit sexual content. For example, an eighth-grade girl once asked me if I had read *The Perks of Being a Wallflower*. I told her that I had just started it. She described it as "raunchy" (there was some sexual content involved, including homosexual acts). It is actually one of the more realistic views available of teenage life, and many teen reviews found on the Internet about this novel agree. The fact is that it is realistic because it includes the sexual experiments and fantasies of a normal teenage guy. Obviously, this realism may be more than some readers want.

You may also want to lie in the other direction. For the middle school or parochial school students, you may choose to omit the fact that there is a mention of sex. Most parents won't disapprove of or pick up the book their child is reading, and most teenagers won't be discussing what they read with their parents. Most of the sexual content in YA books is just a quick mention that it happened. If you want them to read or know about a particularly great book (especially one that might not be approved of by those involved with your audience and especially if the offending material is insignificant), then leave out the sex and drugs. If you are not comfortable with the content, don't use it. Save those books you really want to use but are worried about—use them with an older audience or wait for a request for which they are appropriate.

So I am lying a little when I say that you should lie a little. The fact is that in booktalking you will most often be telling the truth. You will just happen to phrase things ambiguously on occasion. You do not want any fellow librarian or teacher or parent or student to accuse you of lying about a book or anything else. You do not want to lose the audience's trust. But if you use this technique they will recall your actual words and find that they are true in the context of the entire book. Teens can be a smart crowd and they will get the joke.

REFERENCES

Bromann, Jennifer. 1999. "The Toughest Audience on Earth." *School Library Journal* (October): 60–63.

Morris, Holly, and Nicole Eaton. 1999. "Why Johnny Can't Stop Reading Books." *U.S. News & World Report* 127 (August 9): 66.

Munson, Amelia H. 1950. *An Ample Field: Books and Young People.* Chicago: American Library Association.

The Random House College Dictionary. 1980. New York: Random House.

Reid, Rob. SLJ Article. E-mail: *bromannj@hotmail.com* from *reid@ifls.lib.wi.us* (October 18, 1999).

Thomas, Rob. 1997. *Slave Day.* New York: Simon & Schuster Books for Young Readers.

Wilson, Brian. Conversation with Jennifer Bromann. July 9, 2000.

BOOKS FOR TEENS MENTIONED IN THIS CHAPTER

Chbosky, Steve. 1999. *The Perks of Being a Wallflower.* New York: Pocket Books.

Duncan, Lois. 1978. *Killing Mr. Griffin.* New York: Dell.

Duncan, Lois. 1997. *Gallows Hill.* New York: Delacorte Press.

Esquivel, Laura. 1992. *Like Water for Chocolate.* New York: Doubleday.

Kirn, Walter. 1999. *Thumbsucker.* New York: Anchor Books.

Napoli, Donna Jo. 1998. *Sirena*. New York: Scholastic.

Strasser, Todd. 1996. *Girl Gives Birth to Own Prom Date*. New York: Simon & Schuster Books for Young Readers.

Thomas, Rob. 1997. *Slave Day*. New York: Simon & Schuster Books for Young Readers.

Chapter 4

Seven Surefire Booktalking Methods

METHOD I: SETTING A SCENE

Setting a scene, focusing on a character, hinting at the plot, and setting the mood are four commonly described ways to present booktalks. In this chapter I describe these methods, along with three additional styles that work well with today's teens: asking a question, drawing connections, and reading aloud. Be careful not to overuse any one method during a booktalk. Instead, you'll get the best results if you mix the methods around—your talks will be more interesting and you will reach more members of the audience.

One of the most successful ways to present a booktalk is to select just one scene—it is the best way if you are most comfortable with a plot summary or reading from the book. You don't necessarily have to interact with the students, although it helps. This method is usually a great opener. For *Sang Spell* I begin with: "Let's say you're out hitchhiking. I know you would never do anything like that. You've seen the movies. But you do it anyway, only you pick the wrong guy. He beats you up, takes your money, and throws you out on the street. You wake up in a town that you cannot get out of no matter what you do" (Bromann, 1999, p. 63). You need say no more.

Another excellent scene to use is from the first chapter in *Whirligig*. Say something like: "You're at a party. You are the only one not wearing black and white. Your best friend neglected to tell you that it was a chess party and you were supposed to wear black or white for the human chess game. In fact, you are wearing a brightly colored shirt. If that is not embarrassing enough, this really cute girl comes up to you. You think she's going to hit on you. Instead she tells everyone you're a leech and to stop following her around. You're humiliated. You get in your car. You're drunk. I know none of you in this room would ever be drunk, but let's say you are. You start driving on the expressway. You let go of the steering wheel and get ready to die. You wake up in a hospital. You didn't succeed in killing yourself, but you did succeed in killing someone else" (Bromann, 1999, p. 62). Followed by a short plot summary, you've set the hook.

In *Who Killed My Daughter?* Lois Duncan discovers many twists and surprises about her daughter's murder. Focus on the discovery that the man who might have been responsible for her daughter's death closely resembles the fictional hit man pictured on one of the covers of her book *Don't Look Behind You*. The names or nicknames of the two men are even similar. By just pulling out one shocking detail, the students get the idea of what can be found in the book.

There are three ways to set a scene. You can use a short incident that leads into or sums up the story, summarize just one chapter, or choose one significant point in the story. Then one phrase or a few sentences to sum up the plot is all you need.

METHOD 2: ASKING A QUESTION

To use a question when presenting a booktalk, start off by asking the audience a question that relates (even just a little) to the book. This method provokes a discussion on something that relates to the students, leading to a book about the same topic.

Although this method can be one of the best ways to present a booktalk since it involves the students, it can also be overused, becoming obvious and redundant. Use this method when you immediately think of a hot question that will lead them into a fun answer. Use it, too, when you absolutely can't think of anything else to say—you can always think of a question. Just make sure it has to do with the students, and not the book. A question like "What do you think Tommy should do?" is appropriate for a younger level, but middle and high school students don't want any more quizzes. If you want to interest them, don't make them think too much about a book they haven't yet read. Most important, if you ask a question, let them answer. They often want to answer, or hear or share the witty comments of their classmates. If you don't want to deal with their responses, and are afraid they might get out of hand (which they won't), just pose a rhetorical question followed by "Right?" and get their nods instead of conversation.

For *Geeks: How Two Lost Boys Rode the Internet Out of Idaho* I simply ask, "What is a geek?" and wait for their answers. The format for any talk that uses a question should be first to receive responses, next to offer other possible answers, then to reveal the answer according to the book, with an explanation of how it fits into the story or characters. For *Geeks* you might say:

> Well, today a geek is something completely different. These days a geek is someone who is going to make more money than you when they graduate. A geek can never get fired because no one will know how to run the computer system if he's gone. And the school would probably close down if all the computer geeks ditched for the day. That was not a suggestion. *Geeks*, by Jon Katz, tells the true story about two 19-year-old geeks, Jesse and Eric. They never did well in high school and their only friends were members of the geek club, who met in a teacher's room during lunch, since they had no one to sit with in the cafeteria. When they graduated, one worked for Office Max and the other worked on computers for a small local Idaho business. They rode their bikes to work, one quit college because his car broke down and he couldn't get there anymore, and they came home and played Doom and other computer games, downloaded all their music, and talked online to people they never met in person before. Then one day they were interviewed for an article by writer Jon Katz. He made the comment that there were tons of jobs available for people with their skills. Jesse got on the Internet, found out that this was true, and the two of them packed up and headed to Chicago to find jobs and a social life.

This is just one example of how a simple question can tie into everything you need to say about a book.

METHOD 3: DRAWING CONNECTIONS

Drawing connections between pop culture, current events, or real life situations and a book can be an effective way to relate books to teenagers. This method works because the connections you draw are designed to grab the audience's interest and attention.

Relating the Book to Pop Culture

Using pop culture in booktalks mostly involves relating the books to movie, television, and music personalities, or to movies or TV shows themselves. Young adults really get excited when you ask them if they've seen a horror movie instead of if they watched the news last night. They don't often get to share in class what interests them.

When I ask who has seen a horror film like *I Know What You Did Last Summer* to lead into one of Lois Duncan's books, every single hand in the room goes up. This they are not afraid to speak up about, and then they want to know what you are going to tell them about that is like this cool movie that all of their peers have seen. They may not know the answer to an analysis of *A Tale of Two Cities*, but they know all the details of a popular teen movie. You can lead them to more books by mentioning other movies they may have seen based on books, so they think, "That was a book?" Maybe if they knew this great movie came from a book, they might read it, or others like it.

In fact, book sales of Lois Duncan's *I Know What You Did Last Summer* increased after both the movie and video release by the same title. The video even featured an advertisement for the book, just as the new book design advertised the movie (Maughan, 1998, p. 36). If you use a Lois Duncan book, you can mention all the TV movies based on her books. *I Know What You Did Last Summer, Don't Look Behind You,* and *Killing Mr. Griffin* are based on books by the same titles; *Summer of Fear* or *A Stranger in Our House* is based on *Summer of Fear*; *Held for Ransom* is based on *Ransom*; and *I've Been Waiting for You* is based on *Gallows Hill*. Some teenagers remember seeing these movies, others are at least intrigued by the titles. You could do the same with Caroline Cooney's *Face on the Milk Carton,* which was also a made-for-TV movie. Many of today's teens are unlikely to have seen these movie versions, especially those made for TV, but more are likely to be produced. These authors, as well as others, have created plenty of material for movie producers to work with. So many recent movies based on books are appropriate for teenagers. These include *Pay It Forward, The Virgin Suicides, Girl Interrupted, A Perfect Storm, Drive Me Crazy, The Mighty, Interview with the Vampire, October Sky, What's Eating Gilbert Grape,* and many others based on Michael Crichton, Stephen King, and John Grisham novels.

On the SmartGirl.com Web site, teens can submit reviews of books. Many of the books they choose to review are those that have been made into movies. Maybe they choose these because it is all they know, or maybe they really like reading a book based on a movie they really liked. After all, we *always* tell them the book is better.

Relating the Book to Current Events

You can also compare the books to something in the news. They do watch the news or they hear it on the radio, at the dinner table, or in school. Three years after *Driver's Ed* was published, three people in their early 20s were convicted of manslaughter after the stop sign they stole led to a fatal accident (Frankel and Sider, 1997, p. 89). The same incident happened in the book. You can use the example of a teacher convicted of sexual relations with her student and relate it to a book about a crush or relationship with a teacher. This theme is often found in YA literature. *Owl in Love*, *Rats Saw God*, and *Violet and Claire* are some examples. Fiction is often based on reality and reality often imitates fiction.

Relating the Book to Real Life

Books can also be related to something in a teenager's life, such as the miserable school dance or a cheating boyfriend or girlfriend. This is where you can be the most creative and where you have the opportunity to get the most laughs. If you don't know of a situation that actually happened, you can make one up, and throw in the worst things that could possibly happen. For *Like Water for Chocolate* I ask teens to tell me what they would do if they were forbidden to see someone they loved. I then describe what parents might see if they opened the door and witnessed their daughter's unbelievable choice for a date and the car he was going to drive their daughter around in, including a missing door on the passenger's side (Bromann, 1999, pp. 63–64). Although a basic plot summary follows, the talk focuses on this question and the audience's answers compared to what happened in the book.

Teens spend hours on the phone or e-mail or in chat rooms gossiping with friends or boyfriends or girlfriends. If they want to spend this much time hearing the dirt about what is happening with people they know, and even don't know, then it makes sense that they would want to hear the same things about characters in a book. Comparisons become the focus of the talk.

METHOD 4: FOCUSING ON A CHARACTER

You can also focus on a character. Great books almost always have great, memorable characters. Once again, avoid long descriptions of a person. Unless amusing, intriguing, or unique, it is not necessary to detail a character's appearance. Rather, describe the plot, scene, thoughts, or actions by how one person dealt with the situations. Use more action than description. For example, in a book like *These Are the Rules* you can focus on the main character's desire to drive so he can get the girl. For *Stargirl* it may be appropriate to discuss Stargirl's wardrobe, but it is just as important, if not more important, to use examples of her crazy behavior, such as cheering for the other team and singing to people in the lunch room. Your audience can relate to being a unique individual or outcast or being someone who finds a character like Stargirl bizarre. Use a real person or create a stereotypical character that teens are familiar with, describing what he or she may look or act like, to lead into the fictional character from the novel you will discuss.

METHOD 5: HINTING AT THE PLOT

For many books, the plot alone is enough to entice readers. But you want your booktalk to entertain as well, so it feels more like you are telling them about a movie or a real life story than a book. Remember Hazel Rochman's advice: "Your talk is not a plot summary" (Rochman, 1987, p. 28). Of course you can tell them what the plot is or at least hint at it, but you seldom need to make the plot the entire focus. Mentioning what the book is about is often necessary, and some books, like an action-packed adventure story, may be booktalked mostly on plot points. But don't leave it at that. For a few minutes we want young adults to forget that they are hearing about something educational—books.

Hinting at the plot is especially effective for horror or true stories. It can also work well if you speak of a book of fiction as if it really happened. For example, for *The Killer's Cousin* you might say: There was this guy in the news. He was charged with murder. He was acquitted. He didn't do it. But everyone still looks at him like he did. They see his face in the newspaper. Even his family, relatives he was sent away to live with distrust him. He meets the cute girl. He meets the skinhead friend. He meets the psycho cousin. Then he meets his dead cousin.

This kind of short, punchy plot summary can work, but don't overdo it by using it too often or by talking too long. If you don't name the character—at least not right away—it won't sound as if you are talking about someone in a book; it will sound as if you are talking about a real person.

METHOD 6: SETTING THE MOOD

In order to show mood, booktalkers will often use the author's own words, according to Joni Bodart (Bodart, 1985, p. 15). These literal examples may best communicate the mood an author is portraying, but they may not be the best way to present a booktalk. Mood-based talks often include more description than other talks. Long descriptions of scenery, characters, and feelings should be avoided in booktalks; they bore the audience if you are not careful.

Use some creativity to set the mood in your talks. Describing a hostile scene can set the mood for danger. Describing a character's attitude or speaking quickly can set the pace of the book or the behavior of a character. For example, for *Truth or Dairy* I link together funny passages and speak fast to represent the often fast-paced language of a teenager. A funny introduction can indicate a funny book. Some books dictate a somber approach. Books about the Holocaust, murder, and other crimes, for example, might be great reads that require creating and sustaining a serious, respectful mood. Use mood by the words you choose and the way you say them.

METHOD 7: READING ALOUD

Hazel Rochman claims that "the author's own works may be the best lure to the world of the story. Holding the book and reading from it, rather than reciting, avoids the tediousness and strain of memorizing. It also communicates your essential message: The pleasure comes from reading" (Rochman, 1987, p. 7). But even if you read aloud the most interesting passage from a great book, teens will often zone out. This can happen for a number of reasons: some teens don't enjoy being read to, some have a short attention span, and some are visual learners and thus need at least some eye contact; some librarians are not good at reading aloud; and sometimes the audience is just not alert or in the mood.

Amazingly hip for the times, Amelia Munson addresses the topic of reading aloud in *An Ample Field: Books and Young People*, written in 1950. She advises, "The only legitimate time for you to read to a group is when you are presenting material in which the author's style is the important thing and can be communicated in no other way: poetry, some essays, fine writing in general" (Munson, 1950, p. 101). She warns booktalkers to resist the desire to read aloud to be "faithful to the book," and recommends using short quotes or "almost" memorizing the passages as better alternatives. Gillespie and Lembo have similar advice to booktalkers: "Avoid reading aloud unless you are a very good reader, and even then do it sparingly. Reading puts a book between the reader and the listener. In booktalks, as in storytelling, you want to get as close to the audience as possible" (Gillespie and Lembo, 1967, p. 5).

As Munson notes, one time that reading aloud can work effectively is when the author's style cannot be conveyed in any other way. Rap-style poetry is a good example. I have only once attempted to perform a rap from Marie G. Lee's *Saying Goodbye*—in graduate school. I have been hesitant to try in an actual high school because of the language used, but I can see it working in other settings with older teenagers and there is not the danger of parent or administrator complaints. But if you're willing to try it, you can do this yourself (and risk sounding like a fool) or ask for a couple volunteers (and risk the students turning it into a joke). Even if the students first joke about it, they will most likely soon see the serious side. Lee's book contains a few words you might have to replace with "bleep," or you might just use the first paragraph instead, which still includes the word "chink" to demean Koreans. If you use students, maybe one can also make the spitting and breathy mouth sounds used in rap music. The passage to recite is as follows:

All these years it's been something that you're missing,
You think you get away with it when it's us you be dissin',
But from the doors of your stores,
Some chinks gonna be hung,
Or taken care of with a gun.

You call me brother then won't advance me a nickel,
Yellow motherfuckers to blame for their own pickle,
You be chillin' when you take my dough,
Then you put my change down on the floor.

This time, brothers, stand up like we should,
To kick chop-suey asses out of our 'hood.
So watch out for that gun we aim at your yellow throat
When we bust yellow asses all the way back to the boat.
You think dissin' brothers is all fun and games,
Then wave bye-bye to your store—It's all up in flames. (Lee, 1994, pp. 178–179)

Following the reading, you might say something like:

This is one of the songs that is causing many racial problems on the Harvard College campus. Ellen is Korean. Her friend Leecia is African American. Leecia listens to the music, sees it as art, and is part of the group that is bringing rapper Professor T to the school. Ellen is part of the group that Professor T is singing about.

This method could be effective in the right setting and time, and it is an example of a time when a direct quote might be necessary to fully and fairly inform the audience of the book's content. On the other hand, rather than reading the rap aloud, one might prefer to describe the work in general terms, saying that the book uses racial epithets and may be offensive. The booktalker must consider the audience, the setting of the booktalks, the purpose, and his or her own comfort level to determine several possible presentation options for the particular situation.

For *Getting In* I like to recite a section of the book. To do this, I memorize it and then speak as if I am saying it myself, rather than reading it. Consider this passage:

> **If you thought about it, girls and college were a lot alike: there was Early Decision, Regular Admission, and Wait List. The only difference was that with college you took SATs whereas with girls there were all these other examinations you took and failed without even knowing it. It would be nice, actually, knowing what your scores were in life. That way you wouldn't keep trying to ask out Stanford when in probability you'd wind up married to somebody like the University of Las Vegas (Boylan, 1998, p. 14).**

There was no way I could rephrase it as cleverly.

Clearly, there will be times when the best way to convey the author's meaning or humor is through his or her own words. It just should not be a technique used on its own or used as a replacement for the traditional booktalk. In general, reading aloud is almost an easy way out. How hard is it to pick out a passage you liked from a book and read it? Of course, if you have limited time and you're really good, and you know it is the only way to present a book go for it—in moderation. But if you really want to find that hook, dig deeper with yourself to add more to it. Don't *just* read.

REFERENCES

Bodart, Joni. 1985. *Booktalk 2: Booktalking for all Ages and Audiences.* New York: H. W. Wilson.

Boylan, James Finney. 1998. *Getting In.* New York: Warner Books.

Bromann, Jennifer. 1999. "The Toughest Audience on Earth." *School Library Journal* (October): 60–63.

Frankel, Bruce, and Don Sider. 1997. "Dead Stop." *People* 48 (July): 65–66.

Gillespie, John, and Diana Lembo. 1967. *Juniorplots: A Book Talk Manual for Teachers and Librarians*. New York: R. R. Bowker.

Lee, Marie G. 1994. *Saying Goodbye*. Boston: Houghton Mifflin.

Maughan, Shannon. 1998. "I Know What You'll Read This Summer." *Publishers Weekly* (May 18): 36.

Munson, Amelia H. 1950. *An Ample Field: Books and Young People*. Chicago: American Library Association.

Rochman, Hazel. 1987. *Tales of Love and Terror: Booktalking the Classics, Old and New*. Chicago: American Library Association.

BOOKS FOR TEENS MENTIONED IN THIS CHAPTER

Block, Francesca Lia. 1999. *Violet and Claire*. New York: HarperCollins.

Boylan, James Finney. 1998. *Getting In*. New York: Warner Books.

Clark, Catherine. 2000. *Truth or Dairy*. New York: HarperTempest.

Cooney, Caroline. 1990. *Face on the Milk Carton*. New York: Bantam Books.

Cooney, Caroline. 1994. *Driver's Ed*. New York: Delacorte Press.

Dickens, Charles. 1859. *A Tale of Two Cities*. New York: Doubleday.

Duncan, Lois. 1966. *Ransom*. Garden City, N.Y.: Doubleday.

Duncan, Lois. 1973. *I Know What You Did Last Summer*. Boston: Little, Brown.

Duncan, Lois. 1976. *Summer of Fear*. Boston: Little, Brown.

Duncan, Lois. 1978. *Killing Mr. Griffin*. Boston: Little, Brown.

Duncan, Lois. 1989. *Don't Look Behind You*. New York: Delacorte Press.

Duncan, Lois. 1992. *Who Killed My Daughter?* New York: Delacorte Press.

Duncan, Lois. 1997. *Gallows Hill*. New York: Delacorte Press.

Esquivel, Laura. 1992. *Like Water for Chocolate*. New York: Doubleday.

Fleischman, Paul. 1998. *Whirligig*. New York: Henry Holt.

Katz, Jon. 2000. *Geeks: How Two Lost Boys Rode the Internet Out of Idaho*. New York: Villard Books.

Kindl, Patrice. 1993. *Owl in Love*. Boston: Houghton Mifflin.

Lee, Marie G. 1994. *Saying Goodbye*. Boston: Houghton Mifflin.

Many, Paul. 1997. *These Are the Rules*. New York: Walker.

Naylor, Phyllis Reynolds. 1998. *Sang Spell*. New York: Atheneum Books for Young Readers.

Spinelli, Jerry. 2000. *Stargirl*. New York: Alfred A. Knopf.

Thomas, Rob. 1996. *Rats Saw God*. New York: Simon & Schuster Books for Young Readers.

Werlin, Nancy. 1998. *The Killer's Cousin*. New York: Delacorte Press.

Chapter 5

Preparing Booktalks

HOW TO START

Writing a booktalk should begin before you even hold the book in your hand. It starts with book selection. If you plan to talk about more than one book, the process continues as you decide which of the selected books you will actually read. Next is what you think of a book while reading. Finally, you pick up a pen to write a talk.

Force yourself to write something down about each book after you read it. Figures 5.1 and 5.2 show some sample response forms. Joel Shoemaker (a school media specialist in Iowa City, Iowa, and editor of the teens @ the library series) uses these forms after reading a book to make comments for purchasing and booktalking consideration.

Make yourself think of what grabbed you most. If you really have time, write what you might say in a booktalk, even if it is only an idea of what you might use. While reading a book, jot page numbers down with notes for passages or statements that might be useful for a booktalk. Always think "booktalk" while reading. Look for hooks, the things that make you want to keep reading. Who is the most interesting character? What is the central problem or conflict, and is it one to which lots of readers can relate? How (or to what extent) is the problem resolved? What does the protagonist learn? Is there a passage that you had to read aloud? What was the most significant thing about the book that you might tell a friend to interest him or her in reading the book? Do not only look for particular scenes, but think also about what the theme of the talk might be.

You won't always be able to find the best hook right away. It often takes a few days. You may need time to forget the details of the plot, and recall the best parts or be reminded of what mattered most in the

Figure 5.1
Nonfiction Reading Response Form

_____ Quality _____ Popularity _____ Grade Level _____ ©

_____ (Name, date, response #)

Title: Author:

Subject (biog, science, history, etc.):

Content summary:

Scope:

Organization (logical? accessible? interesting?):

Point of view (bias? perspective? expertise?):

Tone (formal? conversational? scientific?):

Appropriateness for intended audience (age, gender, reading level?):

Type of illustrations: _____photo   _____original art   _____black/white

_____color   _____other

Quality Ratings

	Excellent	Good	Average	Poor	Not Acceptable
Accuracy					
Language					
Organization					
Graphics					
Unity, integrity					
Approp. for audience					

Controversial issues or subjects likely to draw reconsideration requests?

(The Big Three: Language [foul], Sex [any], and Religion [almost anything])

Would you include this title in your collection? Why or why not?

book. Sometimes it will hit you right away—the scene you want to use, a character you want to focus on, a news event that reminds you of the book, or a question you want to ask. If it doesn't, wait. Wait a year if you have to. The experiences you have had in a year may help you find a way to better relate to a book. If there is still nothing, maybe you just have nothing to say about the book. Maybe it was good, but not worthy of an excellent talk. Or maybe you'll realize it really wasn't that good, and maybe you don't think your teens would like it either. Let it go. That's OK, too.

There may come a time, though, when you'll need to use some books you've found less inspiring. For example, what if you are asked to speak to seniors in high school and you only have talks prepared for seventh and eighth graders? You may not have time to read more books. In this case, or in a similar situation, when you absolutely need to write a talk for a book and can't think of what to say, consider using the ten steps described in the next section.

Ten Steps for Writing a Booktalk

1. Choose a book that teenagers can relate to. (See Chapter 2 for tips.)
2. While reading, write down notes or page numbers of scenes or words you thought were especially funny or thoughtful. Is there a common theme in your selections? Does one thought lead to a theme that can be expanded?
3. When you are done reading, write down what scenes or phrases you remembered the most. Was anything funny? Sexual? Shocking? Thought provoking? Do these things relate to each other in any way?
4. Ask yourself what questions the book made you think of. Does it remind you of anything you heard in the news? Does it remind you of something that happens frequently in high school like dating, dances, or gossip? What character do you think the teens can best relate to? Why?
5. Read the book jacket and summary. What did the writers of these bits of information think was most important? They often pull out something significant or as an attention getter. True, they may have never read the whole book, or they may be lying, but this will get you to think about a part of the book that was memorable. If you are still stuck, get online or search through your journals and read reviews. What did they write that made you order this book? What

did actual teens like best about the book? Maybe they mention a scene you forgot about or that was memorable to someone else.

6. Start writing. By now you should have enough to write your first sentence at least, whether it is a question, the start of a scene description, a character's feelings, or something from the news or a story that could have happened to any teenager. If you don't know how to start, see "How to Write and Start a Talk Using Styles that Work" on page 78.

7. Let the first sentence lead to the continuation of your opening thought. For example, provide the answer to the question (whether jotting down possible answers, offering the way you want students to respond, or presenting the truth of what happened in the story), or provide the conclusion of the story or the scene (from the media or their lives).

8. Decide whether this is enough information or whether you need to add a plot summary. Most of the time, especially if you open with a question, or with a story you made up or took from a real event, you will have to tell a little about what happens in the book. If you describe a scene or only one aspect of the book that gives the main idea of what happens to the characters, a plot summary is not always necessary.

9. Decide how you will end it. Sometimes this will just be the last phrase in your last thought. Sometimes this is where you will finally mention the title and author, or you can leave them with something to think about.

10. If you can't think of anything at all, then wait. You don't have to write it right away. In fact, sometimes if you wait a few weeks or months, when you sit down to try and write a talk, you'll find it much easier because you'll only recall the most memorable or important parts. Perhaps a thought will come to you and this will lead to posing that thought in your booktalk or using the scene that stayed with you the longest. If you never find that hook, it is OK to give up or use someone else's talks.

Examples

If you are still stuck, following are some examples of how I wrote particular booktalks so you can see how the process works and what kinds of things spark ideas.

- For some books, the right approach will just hit you right away. When I read *Whirligig* I knew I had to tell them about the first scene where the guy leaves a party and causes a drunk driving accident. The rest of the book is completely different. The main character is no longer the party guy and it gets more serious. They will appreciate hearing about the part with the party more than hearing about the part about making whirligigs.
- Some books will remind you of a new teen movie. The plot of John Marsden's *Tomorrow When the War Began* reminded me a little of the movie *Halloween: H20*. In the movie the students all left to go camping while havoc occurred on their campus and in Marsden's book the kids go away to camp and return to find everyone missing in their town.
- For *Hard Love* the thought that hit me was that all problems would be solved if you just didn't let yourself fall in love with someone you can never have.
- For *Violet and Claire* the characters caught in the act of cheating had the most connection for me.
- Sometimes a real life incident will remind me of a book or vice versa. I read *Squashed* at least a year before I wrote a quick talk for it when I needed books that would be appropriate for sixth grade. But that was after I had been to Alaska and on one of the tours they mentioned the record-weight cabbage grown there that year. In the book, a girl grows a huge pumpkin for a local competition. So sometimes future experiences will bring back memories of a book and give you material to write about. You will soon relate everything you see and hear to books and booktalks. Just what you needed in your life.
- For *Geeks: How Two Lost Boys Rode the Internet Out of Idaho* I thought I'd trick them into telling me the old definition of a geek so I could move forward with the new definitions as explained by Katz and try to make the true geeks feel better by letting them know what great things life may have in store for them.
- For *Joy in Mudville: A Little League Memoir* I kept marking and being shocked by the descriptions of cruel little league coaches and parents. The idea was to shock the audience with these facts as well.
- For *Truth or Dairy* I kept marking all the funny passages and calling up my family to read them aloud. I knew I needed to portray the humor of this book in a booktalk by linking several of these examples together.
- Sometimes it is more difficult to come up with what you will want

to say when you did not like the book. Although I am not a fantasy or science fiction fan, I still force my way through some of these books to make myself more aware of what is available. I barely made it through *leo@fergusrules.com*. A virtual world has no interest to me. But still, I thought the fact that this girl who is ugly and who no one likes, who escapes life through the computer and can be a completely different person online, could easily be related to teens, and so I wanted to try and use that as the theme of the talk.

For some books, even after following "Ten Steps for Writing a Booktalk" and considering my examples, you may still think, "I loved this book, why can't I think of a way to make them want to love it, too?" In such a case, you will most likely want to discard the idea of using that book. If it is one you love, but you can't think of a way to make a middle school or high school student love it, then it is best left on a best-of-the-year list for serious readers to discover on their own. But if you are determined to use it, you might briefly summarize the plot and mix it in with more entertaining booktalks.

How to Write and Start a Talk Using Styles that Work

If you are still not quite sure how to begin writing your booktalk, consider the following guidelines for using the various booktalking methods described in Chapter 4.

- Setting a Scene—Use this method when one chapter, scene, paragraph, or moment is the best part of the book, or when one scene is different from the rest. Choose one that can be easily related to the teens, and that can easily establish the plot without summarizing. Recreate the scene like you are telling something that really happened or pretend that it happened to them. It is not necessary to use exact words. Don't worry about giving away an essential part of the plot—even many movie trailers do this to get an audience. Realistically, only a few students in the class will read that particular book (unless you are presenting books they have to choose from for an assignment), and chances are they will forget every detail but merely remember that they want to read it. Start off with words like "Let's say there is this guy you like . . ." or "You are at a party . . ."
- Asking a Question—This method can always be used as a last resort. Sometimes you will have a great question and that will be all you need to make your talk work. But asking a question is also for

when you can't think of anything else—you can always ask a question. Use a question when you want it to lead into something that relates to or is the opposite of what happens in the book. Begin with a question that focuses on the teenagers, such as "What would you do if your parents refused to let you date this guy . . ." and follow with something like "Well, that is not what Pedro did . . ."

- Drawing Connections—This method is used when you immediately think of something in the news or from the movies, but it can also be used when you can't think of anything else to say about the book and you want to relate it to something going on in a teenager's life. Make up a situation. This is easy to do when the book has to do with relationships or school. Start these talks with "You may have heard of the teacher who is in prison for having the child of one of her students . . ." or "Let's say you are looking for a date to the school dance . . ."
- Focusing on a Character—Use this method mainly when one character is the focus of the story. Focus on him/her and his/her actions, and not on a physical, intellectual, or emotional description. Avoid the first person since it can get confusing. Start with "You . . ." to make the audience relate to the character, or just begin describing the character as if he or she is a real person: "There was this guy in the news . . ." Alternatively you can compare the character to a real person or one you invented.
- Hinting at the Plot—Use this method in conjunction with another method. Alternatively, use it when you can make the plot sound real—don't mention it is a book at first, but describe it as actual events and people. You can also use a shortened version of this style if your purpose is merely to promote a specific subject or list of books that the students must choose from. It is best to preface these talks with another type of talk. Try to find a hook beyond what happens in the book. Begin as you would for a character talk.
- Setting the Mood—Avoid long descriptions. Use phrases that describe something funny or scary, or use quick, short sentences to show the rushed adolescent tone of a character. If the book is funny, start with something funny
- Reading Aloud—Use this method only under certain circumstances. such as when you want to get across a great section and have no better words. Then, memorize well or loosely, use only a quote, or cut the speech short. Avoid using "I," even if it is in the quote, unless your audience is aware or can easily understand that your talk will be like a skit.

WRITING WITHOUT READING

Don't tell, but it is possible to write a booktalk without having read the book. This is one thing that almost everyone says not to do. I do not recommend it, especially not as a regular practice, but on occasion, if you are in a rush, if you know they'll like the newest Marilyn Reynolds or Paul Zindel book and you just haven't had time to read it yet, you can still talk about it. Think of it as similar to telling someone about a movie you want to see, but you have only seen trailers or read a review about it. That is still often enough to interest someone else into going to see it with you.

To prepare you can read descriptions, summaries, and quotes from the book; use what you have already read; read online or print reviews; or just go by the table of contents or title alone. However, remember to check reviews for information on questionable content not appropriate for the classroom. Do not try to give a complete summary this way or you might miss something. Just make it a quick mention.

You can also use this approach when you want to add some books that only a few students will have an interest in. For example, it is often hard to make a fairy tale relate to young adults, and few boys will want to read one. So just quickly say, even if you haven't read them all, "If you like fairy tales—guys don't pay attention to this—and if you like love or romance you can find out what really happened to Rapunzel and Beauty in books like *Zel* and *Beauty*." If the students do ask a question, although most won't, just tell them, "It is in the book." You can also admit you did not read it and say something like, "I didn't read this one. I hate fairy tales, but I thought some of you might like them." You can add "especially the guys," if you choose to tease.

I had read some, but not all the short stories in *When Nobody's Home: Fifteen Babysitting Tales of Terror*. All I did was ask, "How many of you babysit or have babysat before?" Nearly all the hands went up. "Then you won't want to read this book, and you especially won't want to take it with you when you babysit." For this book, that is all that is necessary. You don't have to tell them all the stories, particularly since, even though some of the stories are actually kind of freaky, the students might think your rendition is lame or pretend that it is so they don't look foolish in front of their classmates. If they like horror, if they have ever been afraid of being alone in someone's house, or if they have seen those babysitting movies, this will be enough said.

At the time I used this horror book, it was close to the new year, and I had heard a story on the news that high school students were being hired by agencies for $30 to $100 an hour to babysit on the new year's eve of the millennium. So I also told the students I had heard this and that if they had nothing to do that night, they should look into getting a babysitting job. Things like this can be used to write a talk when you have not read the book. The point is that even though I had not read the whole book, I could pitch it to them in a way that *they* might read it all.

I often skip short stories in a collection if they are by authors or on subjects I don't like. You can still often find something to relate the book to, even if you didn't read it all. Sometimes I just skim over parts of books, especially books with a sports theme. If you choose to skip over descriptions of the plays and the actual game you will still get the main idea. You still know who won. You still know the other plot lines. Isn't that all that matters? Who pays attention to a whole baseball game anyway? Well, maybe the guys. I loved *Joy in Mudville: A Little League Memoir*, but I cared more about the little league and cruel coaches and parents than I did about moments in the history of baseball. So I skipped over a few of those. Most of the sports books for YAs are not only about sports, but about relationships, identity, and decision making.

If you're definitely in a hurry, it is possible, although not recommended, to sneak a peak at the book jacket. Not only do the writers of these blurbs try to engage you with lies and exaggerations, but it has been rumored that they often don't read the whole book, either. Not until after reading *Getting In* did I read the excerpt printed in front of the book. It was the exact scene I had recognized in the first chapter as an attention getter and a great way to introduce the book. I could have written the booktalk from that without reading on. Since I had focused on the same scene, maybe reading the book jacket is not such a bad way to write a last minute talk. The main idea of a book is usually introduced early on, anyway.

Read reviews on amazon.com or other print or online sources, especially those submitted by teenagers. What they pick out as something memorable may be what you need to use to make the book memorable or enticing to others. Use all the reviews you can find. Put all of the bits and pieces together from collected reviews and the book jacket, and then skim the pages, and you have a pretty good idea of what the book is about. Find a hook and then briefly summarize.

I know there will be a huge disagreement about these suggestions, but let's be realistic. In your free time you may love to read YA books, but you probably also have a life. Although some people may find this hard to believe, most librarians have no more hours in their day to sit around and read books than the rest of the working world. Most of you do not have time (especially if you work with preschool through high school students) to read enough new books to cover every grade level and have fresh new talks for each classroom each year. That is why I focus on older grades, believing that most younger children are still readers and that the middle school years are when they tend to stop reading. Limited time is why librarians can rightfully borrow booktalks from other sources, and why they can throw in one or two quick mentions of books they haven't read. Since most of us will have to prepare these booktalks on our own time, you need to learn ways to get them done as quickly and efficiently as possible.

I was recently asked by a librarian new to the profession what sources I use for booktalks or if I write my own. I gladly admitted that I write my own, mentioning the article I'd written and this book, but it shows that others have been taught to rely on these sources. When it comes down to a choice of using someone else's booktalk that is readily available or not doing a booktalk at all because there is no time to prepare, which is better?

Imagine that you've been asked to do booktalks on short notice and have absolutely none on the requested topic or for a particular age group. You go to your booktalking sources but don't feel comfortable with the books you haven't read, they are too long for you to memorize or learn, and you don't just want to get up there and read. Read the published notes or critical evaluations to find out about the book. Consider choosing a poetry book for teens like *The Pain Tree and Other Teenage Angst-Ridden Poetry* or *Behind the Wheel: Poems About Driving*. You can easily write a talk after reading a few poems. Short stories could work, too—only read a few. Read the first half of a book. Go through the shelves and find all the books you have read and think about what you remember about each one. Just pick the really short ones and stay up all night reading them. Or use the techniques mentioned earlier in this section. Again, this approach isn't suggested for every book or for every time you booktalk, but it can be used when you are desperate, when you need a last minute talk, or when you just don't want to read the book.

Sometimes you may also get so excited about a book that you write the talk before you read the book. Here's a hint: reading the book first is probably the best idea. When reading *Kissing the Witch: Old Tales in New Skins* I assumed it was going to be a frog who turned into a princess and later found out that it was actually the "witch" who wanted the kiss.

Another time I wrote a talk for *The Fuck-Up*, which I have yet to read and which I doubt I will ever be able to use because of the title and nature of the book. Here is what I came up with without reading the book:

> I probably shouldn't have brought this book. I can't even really tell you what the title is. But luckily the title kind of wraps around the cover, so I don't have to show the other side for you and I can just hold it up and you can kind of see if you can figure it out for yourself, but only for a second. I'm not going to be the one to tell you what it is or they might not let me back here. I might even get fired. Just because of the title I can't even buy it for the library, so you'll have to ask me to order it for you from somewhere else. Only no other library will buy it either. I can't really even tell you the name of the author since I can't pronounce it, but if you do want to know about what happens to this guy who pretends to be gay to get a job, then see me later. Just don't use this one for your book reports. And I don't even have to worry that you will, since you'll never see a copy unless you buy one. And then you wouldn't be able to go to the movies because you would have used your money for this book and I know you wouldn't do that, so I'm not worried at all.

You would have to be very daring, secure in your job, and in a very liberal and open-minded school or public library to use this one. It is just another example of the kind of approach you can take if you did not read the book. In this case, you could focus more on the controversy than the plot. There is a brief plot description on the book jacket.

For *Worst-Case Scenario Survival Handbook* I didn't read all the survival tips, but looked through the table of contents to choose the ones that would be the most interesting in a booktalk. You could do this for any nonfiction book.

Yes, I did read the sources for all the booktalks I wrote for this book, except for a few stories in *When Nobody's Home: Fifteen Babysitting Tales of Terror* (I scare easily) and the sections I skipped in *Joy in Mudville: A Little League Memoir*. But if I hadn't read them, does it really matter? Is that the point? The point is getting the kids to read them, and if you can succeed in that without reading every book, then so what?

KEEPING IT SHORT

Keep the booktalks short. Try to fit in about eight to ten books in 15 to 20 minutes. You will need to spend more time on some books, but balance those with others that you want to mention but not dwell on. Al-

Figure 5.2
Fiction Reading Response Form

_____ Quality _____ Popularity _____Grade Level _____© (Name, date, response #)

Title: Author:

Genre:

Hook?

List and briefly describe main characters:

Mood/tone:

Plot summary:

Conflict/problem:

Climax/resolution:

Theme:

Intended audience (age, gender, reading level?):

Best scene (or favorite quote) for booktalk or readers' advisory:

Any other special (unique, interesting, strange) characteristics of the text?

Controversial issues or subjects likely to draw reconsideration requests?

(The Big Three: Language [foul], Sex [any], and Religion [almost anything])

Would you include this title in your collection? Why or why not?

though most students will love the interruption of their regular routine, remember that some do want to get their homework done or get some computer time in before class ends, so don't take up all the time. Teachers will also often appreciate that you don't use their whole class time, especially if your visit has been arranged by a principal or someone else.

Check out Nancy Keane's Web site, "Booktalks Quick and Simple" (*http://rms.concord.k12.nh.us/booktalks/*), where over 750 short booktalks for all ages from many different writers and for many different books appear. The key is that they are all short. If there are so many of those quick ones out there, then there must be something to it. None of my written talks ever exceed one double-spaced page, and many are only a few lines long, although many become longer when spoken aloud. Bonnie Kunzel of the Princeton (New Jersey) Public Library considers her books as "commercials" and makes them all short (Kunzel, 2000, p. 80).

It is preferable to have short talks, so if a student is not interested in one, it will be over soon, or if you fail to amuse or enthrall them as you had hoped, you don't have to suffer either. But just because a talk is short that doesn't mean it will stay that way. Often the comments of the students not only lengthen the discussion of a book, but spark more ideas to share. Their interest leads you to what you need to talk about next. If they really seem interested in a book, offer more details about whatever they gasped or laughed at. You will get the cues from your different audiences. It is impossible to know ahead of time everything that will work with each group of students.

Practice

While accomplished booktalkers may debate book selections and styles, any booktalker willing to be observed by other adults will agree on the need to practice. You can practice in a wide array of ways, including into a tape recorder, in front of a mirror, to yourself, to your children, to a teen who comes into the library, to your teen advisory board, to a colleague, and in your car five minutes before you arrive at school.

Mentally or verbally rehearse what you plan to say. Visualize success. Read it out loud and make sure it sounds like what you had in mind. Be sure that it makes sense and that it connects. Try to make it sound like natural conversation. What kinds of reactions do you want from people? See if you get them from your practice audience.

It is not necessary to memorize a booktalk, but the more you practice the better you will be at relating what you want to say in the order you want to say it. Practice over and over again until you leave nothing out that you intended to say, even though it may always be with different words. It is not necessary to memorize word for word; you can ad lib. The words may come out different every time, but as long as the key elements you want to express are present, that is all that is important. If it sounds like natural conversation, then you are a success.

35 DOS AND 35 DON'TS

The following are some "rules" for booktalking to the reluctant young adult reader—pitfalls to avoid and tips to follow. If you are booktalking to an audience for the first time and are not sure of their interests and abilities, these rules will help you keep their interest.

35 Ways to Lose Your Audience

1. Starting off with a silly character's name. For example, *Baby Be-Bop*, by Francesca Lia Block, is a moving book about the love of two young men. But if you start off with "Baby Be Bop . . ." your audience may only laugh at the name and not listen to the rest. Slip it in somewhere else.
2. Opening up with a book's name. Slip it in at the middle or end instead. If you open with it, they immediately know it is a book, which could tune out nonreaders. Try to get their interest first.
3. Starting with the author. Most of the students will not be familiar with the authors you choose. Tell the author's name last or when you mention the book's title.
4. Using props. This technique may work with the young ones, and even some older ones, but some YAs may find it silly, and you don't want to risk it. Stick with the traditional storytelling method of telling with just your voice.
5. Starting with "This is a true story." Tell them that later. Make them wonder first.
6. Giving them too much information. They get enough in school, so don't weigh down your talk with dates and names. Your talk shouldn't sound like an assignment. Focus on the story if it is historical or factual, and not on the facts, unless you are specifically asked to do so for a class.
7. Starting with a quote. This technique can be confusing, especially if you are quoting a conversation—they won't know who is talking.
8. Speaking in the first person. They do not want to read a book about you, and that is what they will think it is if you

start with "I." Unless you tell them what you are doing or they see you reading the page, they won't be sure you are not talking about yourself. Use "you" instead.

9. Asking a question you don't let them answer. Questions are great—they involve the students. Students like to talk and they don't get to do it much in class. But if you ask a question like "What do you do for fun in a small town?" and don't let them tell their creative stories, you missed the point of the question. They might even keep thinking of the answer to themselves instead of listening to you. If you don't have time to let them answer or are afraid of what they might say, use something like "In a small town, you probably sit on your porch and talk all night, or walk the streets waiting for curfew, right?" and get no and yes replies instead of full answers. Then lead into a book like *Whitechurch*.

10. Trying to be lyrical. Booktalking is your perfect chance to be creative. But don't tax your muse here by starting with something like "The sun went down early that day, no one knowing it would never rise again. No one knowing that they might not wake up." Save this for your novel.

11. Making references to books they probably haven't read. If as a school librarian you know they are familiar with a certain book or if you know what books were assigned in class, this technique might be useful. But remember that most teens do not read on their own. They probably won't know what you are talking about, and they might even feel left out if they haven't read it.

12. Making references to authors. Avoid this technique for the same reasons mentioned above. Instead, say something like "Maybe you read something by _____" or "Maybe you've seen the movies based on Lois Duncan's books" or, if you are visiting a school, "I see you have some of Caroline Cooney's books in the library here."

13. Sounding like a book jacket. I have read some great booktalks that are really interesting, but they don't transfer into verbal communication. Watch that what you write has the effect of a storyteller or a comedian and not a book jacket. Read your words out loud and make sure your talk sounds like something spoken naturally and not something

that was written. Strive to make it sound like the words just came off the top of your head without planning.

14. Using the word "everyone." Instead of saying "Everyone has heard of . . .," say "You might have heard about . . ." or "Some of you may have heard . . ." Otherwise, they will feel stupid for not knowing what you are talking about, or they'll think you are an idiot for thinking they should know this at their age. We can try, but we can't know everything they know or like.

15. Asking too many questions. A few are fine, but don't give them a list of questions to think about or answer. There is not enough time.

16. Mentioning self-help books. You do not want to insinuate that anyone in that room has a problem of any kind, unless, of course, it is as a joke. Instead, use books that will appeal to a wide range of students.

17. Asking a question about something no one would ever relate to or think about. For example, "Did you ever imagine what it would be like to fall through a hole in the subway and enter the 22nd century where everyone else is a robot?" Uh, no. Or "Did you ever think about how horses give birth?" Probably not.

18. Lecturing, especially on such topics like AIDS or STDs. This is not your job.

19. Assuming they know something. Don't say "You have heard about what happened in Kosovo." Do not assume they all follow all the news. Instead, say "Did you hear about what happened . . ." or "You might have heard about what happened . . ."

20. Relying on their senses. Books can make you aware or make you feel, but if they haven't read the book, don't ask if they can touch, smell, feel, or taste something.

21. Asking a trick question. Don't try and humiliate anyone here. People often get embarrassed if you trick them into saying something wrong. Teasing is one thing, making someone appear foolish is another.

22. Using phrases from your past that they might not understand.

23. Starting with a question or statement geared to only one group. For example, avoid saying "If you like swimming . . ."

24. Making odd noises or sound effects. You may give an excellent impression of an alien, but they might not see it that way, and even if they find you convincing, they may not want to admit it and look like the dork in the room.
25. Ending with a question. You want to move on quickly to the next book, so don't encourage lingering thoughts. Instead end with a quick short sentence and move on.
26. Asking them to think about something scary, such as rape or the death of a parent. You can use these subjects in a talk, but don't ask them to imagine being in these situations.
27. Asking questions related to the book. Don't use something like "Do you think Amy went with Todd or did she stay at home for the summer?" Make them think about themselves and what the book has to do with them instead.
28. Showing too much enthusiasm for the author or book. They do not want to read books you are interested in. So don't say, for example, "I couldn't put this book down." I know that will be hard sometimes, but let them make the judgment about the book.
29. Acting like a news reporter or radio announcer. Say "Do you remember that story in the news . . ." instead. Reality is better than fiction here.
30. Mentioning sensitive topics. Love and weight are definitely issues associated with young adults, but saying something like "You know how great love feels . . ." will make those who were never in love feel worse.
31. Relating personal stories. They don't want to hear about your life.
32. Starting with a diary or letter. They really won't know who you're talking to or what you're doing unless you preface it with something else first.
33. Pretending to be another character, especially someone they know or a celebrity or historical figure. Unless you can pull it off well enough to be believable.
34. Saying something like "This is a book for the good readers in the room." Don't make any of the students feel inadequate—if they are not good readers or if they are not interested in the book or books you talk about. Most teens will assume they can't read a book that's only for the good readers.
35. Reading out loud, unless absolutely necessary.

35 Ways to Hook Your Audience

1. Laugh and Smile.
2. Walk in confidently. Don't let their glares intimidate you.
3. Bring a bookmark listing the titles you're going to talk about. Sometimes you'll see them made into paper airplanes, but you'll see some bookmarks again in the library. Mention that the bookmarks are also available in the library in case they "lose" theirs.
4. Talk about what you know they know. Don't try, however, to relate something to them if you don't have a clue about what interests them.
5. Avoid personal prejudices. You can't like every book, and they won't like each book you like. So try taking a variety of books, even some you don't like.
6. Choose books for the right audience. If you are talking to a high school and you have only read YA books, try reading a few adult books about college students. If you are visiting a parochial school, avoid inappropriate themes.
7. Practice. Some people only practice three times. Some don't practice at all and just take notes with them. Some just say whatever they remember about the book. And some practice over and over again. Practicing is different from memorizing; practicing will mean you don't have to memorize.
8. Follow their lead. If you see they are not interested in something, cut it short, even if you spent hours on that talk and you are only one-fourth through.
9. Cover yourself. If they comment negatively about something you said just say something like, "I know, isn't that weird?" You have to make them think you agree with them.
10. Borrow other people's talks. I know you are supposed to read the books and booktalks and write one in your own style, but you don't always have time. So use another talk for one you've read or make it brief for one you haven't. Don't do all of your talks this way, but a few won't harm anyone.
11. Pretend you don't care if they read or not. Teenagers will do what they are told not to do. I don't mean you should say "Don't read this book. It is awful," but rather something like "Now this is 300 pages, so you probably won't have time for a book about this screwed up guy."
12. Keep in touch with what they want. Know the TV shows,

movies, and music they like, as well as popular trends, but be aware that things go out of style quickly.

13. Talk about what they know, such as what they see on TV or in the movies.

14. Recognize that they are listening if they comment to each other, volunteer, or answer a question.

15. Lie and hint. Stretch the truth a little, especially when the topic of sex is or isn't involved in any way.

16. Ask questions about them. "What would you do?" Everyone likes to talk about himself or herself.

17. Cheat. Read the back of the book like they do. Read a magazine article on the newest boy band you've never heard of and pretend you listen to them.

18. Let them know how *they* can "cheat". Mention those short books and why they are shorter than they appear.

19. Let them talk. They will comment to each other, especially if you bring up a topic in which they are interested. That just shows that you found the hook. After a few seconds or minutes I will nod and wave my arms and just start talking again. They'll fall back in for the next one. They love to talk and gossip and comment and they don't often get to do that during a school day, so showing them that you allow that behavior makes them more comfortable with you and what you are doing.

20. Work on the teacher's or school librarian's time schedule, even if it means starting work a little early. You'll survive.

21. Bribe them. Offer food or entertainment or community service and sneak in the booktalks.

22. Use your hands or other body language. A wink here, a bounce there.

23. Talk to them like they are adults who want to be there and not students.

24. Make it short. Most teens have a short attention span. If it is too long, they will lose interest. There are exceptions, and maybe a long booktalk about a really interesting subject will work, but generally, the audience will drift off for at least part of it if it is too lengthy. Who pays attention to a whole lecture or sermon? And who pays attention to a short comedy skit or a joke? Remember that you can fit more in if you have short talks, and many talks will get longer from the student responses. You can always add more about the book if you see they are really interested in a particular one.

25. Use a variety of books. Sneak in some for all genders, ethnicities, and interests.

26. Tease. Pick a student to be the focus of a comparison with a book character.

27. Choose books they might have heard of. These might be books that have been the basis for popular movies or books mentioned in teen magazines. If you mention titles they recognize, they are more likely to stay tuned in and pay attention to other titles too.

28. Mention in your introduction that you know they don't have time to read and that these books are suggestions for such times as when they have to read a book for school or when they are going on a trip.

29. Understand that perhaps nothing will work for some students.

30. Ad-lib. If they seem interested in a book, keep talking. Tell them whatever else you remember.

31. Use books you haven't read. Don't do this all the time, but if you want to mention a book that you haven't read and you know the hook you would use anyway, it won't matter every now and then. Think of it as similar to wanting to see a movie but you have only heard about the plot or who is in it or that it is based on a Jane Austen novel you loved. You don't necessarily need someone who has seen the movie to tell you about it to make you want to see it.

32. Tell them about books appropriate for their level. Not too old for them, not too young.

33. Use words teenagers use. For example, young women don't describe a guy as "handsome." Instead, they will use a word like "hot." This terminology changes, so keep up with how they are describing men today, and other language they use. Don't overdo it. They'll notice if you are trying to look cooler than you are.

34. Talk mostly about contemporary books. Avoid older books unless they have timeless qualities. Even though some of Lois Duncan's books go back to the 1960s, for example, they are still being made into movies, and horror is always popular. Others are not.

35. Treat them like a friend. Act toward them the way their friends do. Try to avoid punishing or scolding during this time.

REFERENCES

Bromann, Jennifer. 1999. "The Toughest Audience on Earth." *School Library Journal* (October): 60–63.

Kunzel, Bonnie. Booktalks. E-mail *bromannj@hotmail.com* from *BKUNZEL@aol.com* (November 26, 2000).

BOOKS FOR TEENS MENTIONED IN THIS CHAPTER

Bauer, Joan. 1992. *Squashed*. New York: Delacorte Press.

Block, Francesca Lia. 1995. *Baby Be-Bop*. New York: HarperCollins.

Block, Francesca Lia. 1999. *Violet and Claire*. New York: HarperCollins.

Boylan, James Finney. 1998. *Getting In*. New York: Warner Books.

Clark, Catherine. 2000. *Truth or Dairy*. New York: HarperTempest.

Donoghue, Emma. 1997. *Kissing the Witch: Old Tales in New Skins*. New York: HarperCollins.

Fleischman, Paul. 1998. *Whirligig*. New York: Henry Holt.

Gorog, Judith. 1996. *When Nobody's Home: Fifteen Babysitting Tales of Terror*. New York: Scholastic.

Katz, Jon. 2000. *Geeks: How Two Lost Boys Rode the Internet Out of Idaho*. New York: Villard Books.

Lynch, Chris. 1999. *Whitechurch*. New York: HarperCollins.

Marsden, John. 1995. *Tomorrow When the War Began*. Boston: Houghton Mifflin.

McKinley, Robin. 1978. *Beauty*. New York: Harper & Row.

Mitchell, Greg. 2000. *Joy in Mudville: A Little League Memoir*. New York: Pocket Books.

Napoli, Donna Jo. 1996. *Zel*. New York: Dutton Children's Books.

Nersesian, Arthur. 1999. *The Fuck-Up*. New York: Pocket Books.

The Pain Tree and Other Teenage Angst-Ridden Poetry. 2000. Boston: Houghton Mifflin.

Piven, Joshua and David Borgenicht. 1999. *Worst Case Scenario Survival Handbook*. San Francisco: Chronicle Books.

Tangherlini, Arne E. 1999. *leo@fergusrules.com*. Wellfleet, Mass.: Leapfrog Press.

Wittlinger, Ellen. 1999. *Hard Love*. New York: Simon & Schuster Books for Young Readers.

Wong, Janet S. 1999. *Behind the Wheel: Poems About Driving*. New York: Margaret K. McElderry Books.

Chapter 6

In the Schools

GETTING THERE OR GETTING THEM TO YOU

Whether you are in a public library or in a school library, booktalking to kids usually means reaching out to teachers since kids are in classrooms.

If you're in a public library, you begin by contacting someone in the schools. If you are a school librarian, then you can easily start with the teachers. In either case, it is usually best to start with the teachers, but not always easy. Usually you will want to talk with several teachers at each school, and teachers often do not have easy access to telephones during the school day. For them, talking in the evening may be the only realistic option. If possible, provide your home number, or if you are a public librarian, mention when you will be working in the evening. Many teachers won't respond promptly to a call or a letter—especially if they don't know you or why you are calling. Try to be as clear as you can in your message or letter.

If you are a public librarian, school librarians may be an excellent first contact. They understand what you have to contribute. Through them you may be able to reach all the classes, since many schools still have scheduled times for classes to visit the library. School librarians may even want to collaborate. Finally, some principals will prefer that you go through them to arrange the visits.

Most contacts will not respond to a letter, but if you do write, mention that you will call to follow up. You might want to list your qualifications, experience, and the benefit you've seen booktalks provide. If you have been in this particular school before, remind them of the response you previously received from their classes. Let them know that you have a flexible schedule and can accommodate their class whenever they have available time, such as close to the end of a semester or holiday break.

Some schools will view your visit as a burden rather than a benefit. There may be paperwork, forms, and permissions to complete to allow your direct contact with students. School librarians may already frequently present booktalks in the classrooms, so teachers may not need or have time for a public librarian to visit. Or they may not appreciate the disruption of lessons and activities.

Be persistent. If one person doesn't seem interested or doesn't return your call, contact someone else. But if you get no positive response, don't be afraid to give up and try again next year when a new teacher, librarian, or principal might have joined the staff. After all, you should not spend excess time calling and sending letters when there is obviously no current interest. Instead you might want to try another approach. Work through the PTA and have them sponsor a program for parents or teachers about YA books or booktalks. Present booktalks for parents and teachers at meetings or workshops. Such programs will not only give them ideas of new books available, but will make them aware of your availability and what you can provide to their students.

Look for opportunities for more practice while allowing you to spread the word about YA books. Try schools near where you live. Offer your services to other teachers you know or to other programs (such as a juvenile detention center or hospitals) that might welcome a visit.

You will have to work on their time schedule. Get in there when you can—even if it means doing an all-day talk, visiting on several days to reach each classroom, or even visiting on your own time. Our new high school librarian suggested that I present talks during their homeroom, as the teachers at their school don't do much during this time anyway. The students may not appreciate such a suggestion—this is probably their gossip time to share the last night's phone and e-mail conversations or what happened on their favorite TV show. If a similar situation is your only opportunity, shorten your talks or limit the number of books you use so that the students still have time for themselves. If an assembly is your only chance, it is not as bad as it sounds—think of yourself as a motivational speaker, not a librarian. Avoid the lunchroom talks, however; students will not be pleased if you disrupt their only time to talk loudly with their friends. Eventually the schools or teachers will start asking you to come in. Then you can be more selective and have more control over your schedule.

If you can't get to them, invite the students to come to you. Bribe them with food, or another activity afterward. Jenny Wegner, the children's and young adult librarian at Oak Creek (Wisconsin) Public Library has a monthly program for young adults, "Books, Food, and Fun,"

Each month she booktalks before she feeds them, gives them a craft to make, and/or has a visitor entertain them. An amazingly high number of sixth, seventh, and eighth graders attend this after-school program by choice. Mostly they come for the food and for something to do after school, but the books get promoted, too. I'm all for trickery and bribery.

PREPARE TEACHERS FOR YOUR VISIT

Poor communication between you and the teachers or librarians in the classrooms or media centers you visit can spell disaster. They may speak up about how important reading is—which may not be the approach you are taking and which is exactly what turns off most teenagers. Think about it. How many times have teens heard an adult say this? Is saying it one more time really going to convert anyone into a rabid reader? Is it going to motivate anyone who hates reading to change suddenly?

Once I went into a classroom and the teacher told the class that they might decide they, too, want to become librarians. "What?!" I was in shock and did an Ally McBeal move in my mind, tackling the teacher to the ground before she could continue. I can almost guarantee none of them will become librarians. This was a sixth-grade class. Most of them are not thinking of a career. Furthermore, librarians are still portrayed as mean old ladies in glasses and a hair bun, shushing students. Even the teen show *Dawson's Creek* represented the high school librarian this way in one episode. You can change that image for them.

To avoid such fiascoes, provide the teachers—in advance of your visit—with the introduction you would like them to use.

HOW DO YOU KNOW IF YOUR BOOKTALKS WORK?

An evaluation of your work lies in the responses you get in the classrooms, what the students say to you afterward, whether you see them later in the library, and whether the books you talk about get checked out or have waiting lists. As mentioned earlier, your best indication of success is if your audience pays attention without looking away or without working on something else, if they laugh where you intended and more, if they comment to each other about things you've said, and if they participate and play along. You will know you have failed if they just stare at you and don't laugh or smile or participate, if they are looking around or down at a book, if they are writing, if they are holding their own conversation in the middle of a summary or at an inappropriate time, if no one volunteers an answer, if you never see them again, and if the books you mentioned never get checked out.

There is no need for a formal evaluation form. First of all, it might make *you* feel bad. You want them to think you already know what you are doing. They don't need to grade you. You are the expert. Try giving only the teacher an evaluation form—asking what the students may have said afterward may be a better way to assess your reception

If you do choose to present an evaluation form to the students, use questions that focus not on your presentation, but on the books and the talks. For example, "Which of these books would you read based on what you heard today?" Then you would in a sense know which booktalks worked and which ones didn't. If you need concrete proof of the effectiveness and quality of your talks, get your teen advisory board or summer volunteers to listen to your talks. See how they respond and ask them what they think. They will be more honest, anyway, since they know you.

Some booktalkers insist that an evaluation is the best way to know their strengths and weaknesses. If this is where you stand, look at sample evaluation forms in Patrick Jones's *Connecting Young Adults and Libraries: A How-To-Do-It Manual* (Jones, 1998, pp. 263–264)

A FINAL NOTE

It is possible that I have offended everyone at least once by this point. If I have provoked you to take action or try something new or consider a different approach, then that is all that matters. So many people are booktalking out there and presenting great booktalks. Every one of them has his or her own style. If you already have an approach that works for you, then I hope you found this book entertaining or that it gave you a few new ideas to try. If you have felt clueless and thus never booktalked or if you have tried booktalking and wished it had been more successful, then I hope you will try some of the approaches outlined here—they may be what you need to do to be successful.

Many of you may disagree with my philosophy on booktalking. My thoughts are that most teenagers, especially reluctant readers, don't have time to read or don't want to read (because it is not the thing to do or because they would rather do other things). But if you give them what they want and what they see in the movies and in their lives, and if you make every part of your talk fast, lively, and fun, maybe they'll think reading and the books you mentioned are fun, too. Joni Bodart's dissertation findings show that booktalks can make students interested in the books at hand, but not necessarily have an effect on reading attitudes

(Bodart, 1987, pp. 93–94). Don't expect to have an effect on every student, but when all the students are listening and laughing rather than rolling their eyes, looking at their homework, or watching the clock, you know that you have their attention. They may not pick up a book, but they also may not think reading and the library are so bad after all. At least they won't see you as the stereotypical librarian or whisper to their friends about how lame you are. If you can capture their attention, that can lead to a more comfortable rapport when they are in the library and need your help.

Remember that booktalking is not just about getting kids to like the books *you* like. It is not just about getting them to read. It is about making them see that reading is OK. Even if they don't read on their own and even if they don't have time to read at this point in their lives, they might see why others do it and how it can be fun or meaningful.

I have read many booktalks that break my rules, but if they didn't work for their writers then they probably wouldn't keep using them and putting them out there for others to read. Every community and teenager is different, and the material in this book is all just guidelines and suggestions. Do what works best for you. I know this approach works perfectly for me, but maybe your way works perfectly for you. Use some of these ideas, or ignore everything and go with tradition. You are free to disagree with me, as I disagree with others. You don't have to use what I say verbatim, but make up your own talks and soon you will be able to write a booktalk for every book you touch. You'll just have to try it for yourself to see what happens next.

REFERENCES

Bodart, Joni. 1987. *The Effect of a Booktalk Presentation of Selected Titles on the Attitude Toward Reading of Senior High School Students and on the Circulation of These Titles in the High School Library.* Denton, Texas: Texas Woman's University.

Jones, Patrick. 1998. *Connecting Young Adults and Libraries: A How-To-Do-It Manual*, 2d ed. New York: Neal-Schuman.

Part II

Ready-to-Present Booktalks

Although these booktalks are written, they are not intended to be followed verbatim. They are just guidelines of the main points and the introductions to be used. Every time a talk is used it should be different, depending on student response, the time available, and the booktalker's memory. These talks may appear short but they will seem longer to your audience when they are actually spoken aloud. Length will be based on responses, participation, and the booktalker's understanding of the audience's interests. The introductions are hooks that usually remain somewhat the same, but the summaries or descriptions of the book may change in response to the audience.

SAMPLE BOOKTALKS FROM THE AUTHOR

Note: Keep in mind that recommended grade levels refer to both the typical interest level and the appropriateness of mature subject matter; a recommendation is in no way intended to prescribe who will be interested in reading a particular book. This book focuses on young adults ages 12–18, so booktalks are only identified for Grades 6–12 even if they are appropriate for a younger or older audience.

BOOKTALKS USING MY STYLES

Anderson, Matthew T. 1999. *Burger Wuss*. Cambridge, Mass.: Candlewick Press.
Realistic
Grades 7–9

Somehow you managed to get the popular, pretty girl who somehow got the idea that you're funny and adventurous. Then one night you're at a party and you see her with another guy. She doesn't care. And he just smiles. There is nothing you can do but get revenge. So you know this guy works where your ex used to work at O'Dermott's—the burger joint. That's how they met. You take her place and naturally someone's going to get hurt in *Burger Wuss*, by Matthew T. Anderson.

Banks, Melissa. 1999. *The Girls' Guide to Hunting and Fishing*. New York: Viking Press.
Realistic
Grades 11–12

You know that rules book that tells women how to get a man. Guys, you'll have to close your ears for a few minutes so I don't give away any of our secrets. Well, there are also a couple books about rules for girls—*The Rules for Teens*, by Meg Schneider, and *The Real Rules for Girls*, by Mindy Morgenstern and Amy Inouye. I am sure none of us in this room has ever tried any of the tips from those or from magazines about how to get a guy to like you. But let me tell you about this girl. She is out of college and a failure with men, so she decides to give the rules a try. Rule #1 Don't call him. #2 Don't accept a date less than three days before. Rule #3 Be feminine. Rule #4 Don't be funny. How many of you do all that? This guy amazingly keeps calling. Then she sees him with another woman, so she goes out with another man. He's gets kind of upset and doesn't call. She throws out the rules and might have to add another guy to her list of failures in her book *The Girls' Guide to Hunting and Fishing*, by Melissa Banks.

Bates, Michael. 1995. *Gorgeous*. New York: Bantam.
Horror/Suspense
Grades 8–9

There is this girl and she somehow manages to get the best looking guy in school as her boyfriend, or maybe you're that guy that chose her. But he breaks up with her and starts dating her best friend. She said she was over him. She's not. All she ever does is think about him and getting him back. Then she and her friends break into a cosmetics lab on a school trip and discover a secret cream that doesn't just make your skin flawless, but it can actually change the shape of your nose or cheekbones. Forget plastic surgery. Only soon something starts happening to her skin in the places where she and her friends put the cream. Someone is out to get you and turn the most popular girls in school into the ugly freaks of the school in *Gorgeous*, by Michael Bates.

Bauer, Joan. 1992. *Squashed*. New York: Delacorte Press.
Realistic
Grades 6–8

You might have heard on the news about the biggest cabbage grown in Alaska last year (substitute any national or local prize for that year, although most students will have no clue what you are talking about anyway). Well maybe you didn't. Anyway, it weighed in at 91.6 pounds. That's about as big as some of you in this room. They do have sunlight until at least midnight for most of the summer up there. Well, you are probably never even going to pick an apple off a tree, so I doubt you'll be growing any vegetables. And this all might seem kind of silly. But winning the prize for the biggest pumpkin at the state fair is more important to

Ellie than going to a movie with her friends. She would make herself sick to save her pumpkin from the weather and thieves in *Squashed*, by Joan Bauer.

Block, Francesca Lia. 1998. *I Was a Teenage Fairy*. New York: Joanna Cotler Books.
Fairy Tale/Fantasy
Grades 9–10

You have probably made wishes on stars before, thrown pennies into mall fountains. (You could also start off by asking them what they would wish for if they had the chance.) You might touch the clock with your finger at 11:11 and twist your friend's necklace around when the clasp is in the front and say, "make a wish." Maybe you get lucky and one of these wishes you've prayed for 1,000 times finally happens, but most likely that guy or girl doesn't ask you out. And you still don't wake up with a new car in your driveway. But if you are Barbie in *I Was a Teenage Fairy*, by Francesca Lia Block, you might get lucky enough to have your very own fairy.

Block, Francesca Lia. 1999. *Violet and Claire*. New York: HarperCollins.
Short/Realistic
Grades 9–10

Let's say you're in love with this guy. He may be a bit old for you. He *is* your teacher. And he invites you on a picnic where you frolic barefoot in a fountain. Well, maybe you just walk along the crowded beach or go to a movie or something. But I'm talking about a book here, so I can't make everything fit your perfect date. Anyway, afterwards you kind of get together and you fall for him. Big mistake. Next time you come over, he opens the door and right by your feet are another woman's shoes. You've seen those shoes before. They belong on the feet of a new tall, red-headed someone in your class. You leave crying and run to your best friend who you've barely spoken to since she's made it big and started on drugs after she sold a screenplay at only 17. You both cry but then you do what all women do. You think you can get him back. So you put on your best clothes, fix your hair and makeup, and go over there. Only you are too late once again. This time you see him with your best friend. That is what happens to the friendship of *Violet and Claire*, by Francesca Lia Block.

Block, Francesca Lia, and Hillary Carlip. 1998. *Zine Scene.* Los Ange-
  les: Girl Press.
Nonfiction
Grades 7–11

Take the name of the first pet you ever had and add your mother's
maiden name. That's the last name your mother had growing up. Probably the name of her parents and maybe her name now. (I say this like
they should know, but probably don't.) Anyone want to share? (Answers
may include Fluffy Peterson, Flash Heller). Well, then you have your
title or pen name and are on your way to starting a zine. If you don't
know what that is, it is a minimagazine you create yourself. It can even
be only a page long. It can be free, 10 cents, or you can charge up to
$10. I wouldn't try the $10 unless you've got it on glossy paper with color
photos or something. It can be about you, your pet, your boyfriend, your
job, your favorite object or idol, movies, school, teachers, music, or anything you want to write about. It can be comics or words. Have pictures
or art. Be real or fake. But if you still have no idea what I am talking
about, you can look at *Zine Scene*, by Francesca Lia Block and Hillary
Carlip, for some ideas.

Boylan, James Finney. 1998. *Getting In.* New York: Warner Books.
Adult/College/Realistic
Grades 9–12

"If you thought about it, girls and college were a lot alike: there was Early
Decision, Regular Admission, and Wait List." Don't get any ideas. I'm
just talking about getting a date here. "The only difference was that with
college you took SATs whereas with girls there were all these other ex-
aminations you took and failed without even knowing it. It would be nice,
actually, knowing what your scores were in life. That way you wouldn't
keep trying to ask out Stanford when in probability you'd wind up married to somebody like the University of Las Vegas." So these are Dylan's
problems. Getting into college, as he screwed up the SATs by filling in
the wrong circles and pretends to be the dean of one school, interview-
ing a student, and getting in with the women, which doesn't help that
he invents a girlfriend who soon dies of a monkey bite. Then there are
his friends he is traveling with in the huge Winnebago his uncle rented.
And they are no better. One showed up to his Harvard interview burp-
ing in a backwards baseball cap, sleepy from his late night with the wait-

resses he met. And besides all this, there's a little murder and revenge and a few scenes I can't talk about in this classroom in *Getting In*, by James Finney Boylan.

Cisneros, Sandra. 1991. *The House on Mango Street*. New York: Vintage Books.
Short/Adult/Realistic
Grades 7–12

You probably live on _____ (insert several local street names) street, but if you lived on Mango Street like Esperanza in *The House on Mango Street*, you might wear clothes that don't match or fit, you might get married in seventh grade (say eighth if it is an eighth-grade class), you might be confined to your home, or pay to have friends. And maybe someday you'll get to leave.

Clark, Catherine. 2000. *Truth or Dairy*. New York: HarperTempest.
Humor/Realistic/Romance
Grades 7–10

(Spoken really, really fast, like a teenager). The impossible happens. Your boyfriend breaks up with you just because he is going away to college (moving, if it is to seventh and eighth grade, although I'm sure some may have college boyfriends these days). You stare in the closet, as if there are answers in there, as if he is in there, as if there are clothes you actually like in there. His friends are now your former friends—your enemies. You should have broken up with him first. You wanted to, but you don't break up with people over little things like moving to another town. When you tae-bo in gym glass, you pretend it's his face, and you flail around until the guys' class comes in and sees you. You'll never get another date now. Only there is someone else who keeps hanging around. Almost a stalker. He is always in the parking lot where you work. So he works there too. He was one of those scrawny guys who everyone beat up all the time, only now he's taller and wider and cuter, and he still has the scrawny guy personality, so he doesn't know he's hot yet. And your ex starts calling and writing to you. And you have no idea what to do. Exactly like Courtney in *Truth or Dairy*, by Catherine Clark.

Conford, Ellen. 1998. *Crush*. New York: HarperCollins.
Short Stories/Realistic/Humorous/Romance
Grades 7–10

If you want to ask someone to a dance or get them to ask you, what do
you do? (Wait for answers.) Those would probably all work, but in *Crush*,
by Ellen Conford, the students at Cutter's Forge High School go about
it differently. One tosses a coin over her shoulder and her dream date
appears, another couple might simply cut their fingernails or hair, and
another will be a little sneaky and interview the hot new foreign exchange
student even if he doesn't speak English. But just like in real life, some
will get to go to the dance and others will be staying home that night.

Cushman, Karen. 1994. *Catherine Called Birdy*. New York: Clarion
   Books.
Historical
Grades 6–8

Let's say there is this guy you really like, but your parents won't let you
be with him. You are meant for someone else. It doesn't matter who.
He just has to be the same religion you are or the same color you are.
They hire a matchmaker who keeps bringing old guys, or bald guys, boring guys, mean guys, but no one you'd ever want to see again. (Describe
as many types of disgusting and unappealing men as you can think of.)
What would you do? (Answers may include run away, sneak around, wait
until you find someone you like in your religion.) Well, in *Catherine
Called Birdy*, by Karen Cushman, Catherine is being forced to marry
someone with a little more money or status. Which is not so bad, but
her father keeps bringing her men twice her age. They smell, they're
old, or they're crude. She just has to figure out how to get out of it all,
which wasn't as easy in medieval times as it is today.

Donoghue, Emma. 1997. *Kissing the Witch: Old Tales in New Skins*.
   New York: HarperCollins.
Fairy Tales/Gay/Lesbian/Short Stories
Grades 8–12

You probably think you are too old for fairy tales. You know all the stories by heart already, even if you never remember actually hearing them.

But *Kissing the Witch*, by Emma Donoghue, is a little bit different. I bet you think that Cinderella kissed the prince and married him and lived happily ever after, when it was actually the fairy godmother she kissed and went home with. All these stories are like that. The "true" versions they never told you as a kid.

Duncan, Lois. 1992. *Who Killed My Daughter?* New York: Delacorte Press.
Nonfiction/Mystery
Grades 7–12

How many of you have seen the movie *I Know What You Did Last Summer?* (I raise my hand, too.) Well, we shouldn't have. The author of that book, Lois Duncan, specifically asked us not to see it because of how much violence was added. Her daughter was murdered. (I also show two pictures from the book that compare the physical similarity between the suspected hit man of her daughter and the fictional hit man in her book *Don't Look Behind You*. I tell them about their similar names, as well. I can see the shock on some of their faces. I tell them to check her Web site for updates, and I mention other books of hers that have been TV movies.)

Duncan, Lois. 1997. *Gallows Hill*. New York: Delacorte Press.
Mystery/Suspense
Grades 6–9

(I start off by asking for a volunteer who wants me to try to read his or her mind. I try to pick one of the jokesters of the group.) I see that you hate reading. That you can't wait for school to get out. And oh, I see a girl. (Then I describe a girl who is similar in looks to several of the girls in class so there can be speculation on who it is. If you choose the right student, there won't be any embarrassment, but they will laugh for the fun of it. Expand on predictions.) Well, I'm not really very good at this yet. I just read a book. But in *Gallows Hill*, by Lois Duncan, Sarah is asked to tell fortunes at a carnival, only she finds that she can actually see the future and knows more about people than they want her to know.

Glenn, Mel. 1997. *Jump Ball: A Basketball Season in Poems*. New York: Lodestar Books.
Short/Poetry/Realistic
Grades 7–10

Let's test how well your memory is working today. What were some of the announcements over the PA system this morning? (Hopefully it will be a day of good news. You should also find out if they have announcements or if they post bulletins instead.) Well, at Tower High in *Jump Ball*, by Mel Glenn, the students may hear something like "Memorial service for Steven Walker will be held Friday in the school auditorium. The debate team will compete this afternoon. The music club reminds people to attend the spring concert. Have a nice day." All in one announcement.

Gorog, Judith. 1996. *When Nobody's Home: Fifteen Babysitting Tales of Terror*. New York: Scholastic.
Horror/Short Stories
Grades 7–9

How many of you babysit or have babysat before? (Nearly all the hands go up). Then you won't want to read this book, *When Nobody's Home: Fifteen Babysitting Tales of Terror* and you especially won't want to take it with you to read when you babysit.

Haddix, Margaret Peterson. 1997. *Leaving Fishers*. New York: Simon & Schuster.
Religious/Realistic
Grades 6-9

Schools are filled with geeks, freaks, jocks, hippies, preps. What else? Help me out here. What kind of cliques do you have at this school? And they usually sit together at lunch or hang out in the halls or after school or on the weekends, right? In the book *Leaving Fishers*, by Margaret Peterson Haddix, there is a different group: The Fishers. These kids are hated even more than the nerds of the school. No one will sit with them at lunch. But Dorry is new to school and they are the only people who will talk to her. She doesn't notice that anything is different about them until they start to pray at lunch. Before she realizes it, the parties and fun turn to Bible study and work, and she has found herself in a cult that she can't get out of.

Hill, David. 1997. *Take It Easy*. New York: Dutton Children's Books.
Adventure/Survival
Grades 6–8

You've seen those talk shows about boot camp for kids, right? (For some reason the teens I work with love this idea of boot camp.) Where "bad" kids get sent away to be screamed at and pushed to the ground and they have to exercise and eat soap until they stop their attitude problem. In *Take It Easy*, by David Hill, a group of students are sent out to hike in the woods. One is there because his mom died, one was sent by the state, one won the trip in a raffle, and one is just rich. It was not meant to be as tough as boot camp until their leader dies on them and they can't find their way out.

Jukes, Mavis. 1999. *Cinderella 2000*. New York: Delacorte Press.
Fairy Tale/Realistic
Grades 7–8

Have you ever asked your parents if you could go somewhere with your friends and they wouldn't let you? Even just to the movies, but they said you had too much homework or it was a school night or "remember what you did to your brother last week?" But it could be even worse. You could be like Ashley in *Cinderella 2000* whose stepmother with wild clothes like _____ (fill in the blank with a currently unfashionable TV or movie star) won't let her go to the big New Year's dance where everyone from school will be that night, especially the guy she's been trying to get together with. Instead you have to stay home and babysit your evil stepsisters. Until someone comes for a visit.

Katz, Jon. 2000. *Geeks: How Two Lost Boys Rode the Internet Out of Idaho*. New York: Villard Books.
Nonfiction/Adult
Grades 8–12

What is a geek? (Answers may include a dork, a nerd, or a person who bites off a chicken's head. Or read aloud definitions from the book instead.) Well, today a geek is something completely different. These days a geek is someone who is going to make more money than you when they graduate. A geek can never get fired because no one will know how to run the computer system if he's gone. And the school would probably close down if all the computer geeks ditched for the day. That was not a suggestion. *Geeks*, by Jon Katz, tells the true story about two 19-year-old geeks, Jesse and Eric. They never did well in high school and their only friends were members of the geek club, who met in a teacher's room during lunch, since they had no one to sit with in the cafeteria. When they graduated, one worked for Office Max and the other worked on computers for a small local Idaho business. They rode their bikes to work, one quit college because his car broke down and he couldn't get there anymore, and they came home and played Doom and other computer games, downloaded all their music, and talked to people they never met in person before. Then one day they were interviewed for an article by writer Jon Katz. He made the comment that there were tons of jobs available for people with their skills. Jesse got on the Internet, found out that this was true, and the two of them packed up and headed to Chicago to find jobs and a social life.

Kindl, Patrice. 1993. *Owl in Love*. Boston: Houghton Mifflin.
Fantasy
Grades 7–10

If there is someone you like, what do you do to find out everything you can about them? (Answers may include memorizing their schedule, finding out their address or phone number, asking friends.) Well, that might be considered stalking in some states *and* some schools (if the students answer with "stalk her or him" as many will, just continue with "And that could be illegal"), especially if it is a teacher you're after. (They will look at their teacher with disgust.) Don't worry. I don't mean your teacher or anyone at this school. But for Owl in *Owl in Love*, by Patrice Kindl, she is in love with her teacher. And since she is a shape-shifter and can turn herself into an owl or a human, she just changes into an owl and perches herself on a branch right outside her teacher's window every night. You might think this is kind of sick, especially because the teacher is short, old, and bald (you may want to change this description if it fits the actual teacher in the room), but owls can only fall in love once, or so she thinks.

Kirn, Walter. 1999. *Thumbsucker.* New York: Anchor Books.
Adult/Realistic
Grades 9–12

Justin is in high school. He still sucks his thumb. So his dentist hypno-tizes him and all of a sudden he stops. Now he needs *other* ways to sat-isfy his oral fixation in *Thumbsucker*, by Walter Kirn.

Krakauer, Jon. 1996. *Into the Wild.* New York: Villard Books.
Adventure/Nonfiction/Adult
Grades 7–12

You've seen the movies. You know what can happen to hitchhikers or the people who pick them up. I've even seen kids hitchhiking to school. This is not a suggestion. But sometimes you wonder if hitchhikers are not carrying a gun ready to rob you and take your car, where are they going or what are they running away from? Christopher McCandless was a real hitchhiker who Jon Krakauer wrote about in an *Outside* maga-zine article and in his book *Into the Wild*. Christopher just graduated college and everyone thought he was ready to go to law school. But in-stead he disappeared for months. His apartment was empty and he do-nated all his money to a charity. He changed his name and traveled west ultimately up to Alaska without a trace. The people who picked him up on the road had no idea that he actually had a college degree, and that he was considered missing by his parents until they saw or heard about the magazine or news article about the man who died in the Alaskan wilderness.

Lee, Marie G. 1994. *Saying Goodbye.* Boston: Houghton Mifflin.
Realistic/College
Grades 7–10

(Have a student rap this excerpt or recite it yourself. There is more, but the language in the other passages might be difficult to avoid. You can also have one or two students making the sounds of rap music with their mouth and hands on the side.)

> All these years it's been something that you're missing,
> You think you get away with it when it's us you be dissin',
> But from the doors of your stores,

Some chinks gonna be hung,
Or taken care of with a gun.

This is part of one of the songs that is causing many racial problems on the Harvard College campus. Ellen is Korean. Her friend is African American. Leecia listens to the music, sees it as art, and is part of the group that is bringing rapper Professor T to the school. Ellen is part of the group that Professor T is singing about in *Saying Goodbye*, by Marie G. Lee.

Littke, Lael. 1998. *Haunted Sister.* New York: Henry Holt.
Mystery
Grades 7–9

Let's say you have a sister. She really annoys you. She takes things from your room. Erases your phone messages. And steals your boyfriend. If you're a guy, maybe she tells your girlfriend *everything* about you. She tells your parents that you are the one who lost the dog and broke the bathroom door. (You may want to add other examples or ask for suggestions.) And that isn't even that bad considering she is dead and doing all this from inside your head. That is what Janine thinks is happening to her in *Haunted Sister.*

Madden-Lunsford, Kerry. 1996. *Offsides*. New York: William Morrow.
Adult/Sports
Grades 9–12

Now the girls in this room know the one thing that is more important to a guy than women—sports. (You can also pose this as a question and see if you get the right response. Chances are it will come up eventually if not first.) You almost need to check the TV guide or surf all the channels before you call your boyfriend, and you'll never get a date for the prom if you call to ask during the Final Four. Liz has learned this fact of life in *Offsides*, by Kerry Madden-Lunsford. Her father is a college football coach and so she's dragged around from one football town to another, ignored by the men who love sports more than her.

Many, Paul. 1997. *These Are the Rules.* New York: Walker.
Realistic
Grades 7–9

All right guys, there is this girl you like. She keeps coming around and asking about you, but spends all her weekends with this older guy with a car who can take her to the beach. You don't even have a license. So you convince your dad to teach you to drive and to lend you his car. You convince this girl to go out with you. But it is a disaster. It rains and you can't get the top down. She goes home in that other guy's car and you drive into a ditch on the way home. Just one of the many problems Colm has in *These Are the Rules*, by Paul Many.

Marsden, John. 1998. *Checkers.* Boston: Houghton Mifflin.
Realistic/Mystery/Short
Grades 7–11

You are in a mental hospital. I don't mean this school. Just pretend. And I don't mean that any of you are crazy. Well, maybe you are. But you are in there because of something you did and something your parents did. It was even in the newspaper. You saw it. And little by little you'll eventually tell us what that is in *Checkers*, by John Marsden.

Alternate talk: There's this girl in a mental hospital. She's there because she killed her dog. Little hints about why she did it are slipped in until you figure it out yourself in *Checkers*, by John Marsden.

McKean, Thomas. 1997. *My Evil Twin.* New York: Avon Books.
Realistic/Humor
Grade 6–8

Sometimes you can't change what people think of you no matter what you do. Everyone thinks you're smart and quiet, you fail a test, and you still get an "A" in the class. People think you're a dork, you come back the next year with new clothes and hair, maybe even a new nose, and no one notices. Or maybe you're an athlete or the coolest kid in school who can't pass a test and when you finally do everyone thinks you cheated. Well, in *My Evil Twin*, by Thomas McKean, Jellemiah John Jensen gets a real chance to start over. His new school gets two of his records from his last school. One has the name he wants to be called,

John, and one has the name his parents call him, Jellemiah. So when the principal thinks he's a twin, he lets him and everyone at school think he is, and he continues to show up some days as the nerdy John, and other days as the cool Jellemiah, who everyone would expect to skip school.

Mitchell, Greg. 2000. *Joy in Mudville: A Little League Memoir*. New York: Pocket Books.
Nonfiction/Sports/Adult
Grades 7–12

How many of you have ever played Little League or tee ball or soft-ball? (Let them raise their hands.) Did you have coaches who wanted you to play for fun, or was winning more important? (Wait for answers.) Maybe you've seen it or just heard it on the news, but sometimes parents and coaches of Little League can get a little out of control. One guy kicked his kid in front of all his teammates after the boy refused to play in a game, a tee ball coach in Oklahoma was sentenced to 12 days in jail for choking a 15-year-old umpire during a game, a 16-year-old umpire was shot at by a coach angered with a call on a close play, and in college baseball, a guy was intentionally hit in the head by a ball and was never able to see out of that eye again. The guy who hit him was recruited by a professional team. *Joy in Mudville*, by Greg Mitchell, tells the story of the kids and parents he deals with while coaching Little League in a New York town where the kids of famous directors and writers live. And in it, he also tells of his experience with baseball growing up, and the cruel stories he has heard of kids, parents, adults, professional players, and coaches who only want to win the game and be the best.

Mosier, Elizabeth. 1999. *My Life as a Girl*. New York: Random House.
Adult/College/Romance
Grades 9–12

This is a situation for the girls. Let's say your friend sets you up on a blind date with her cousin. He picks you up, but when you open the door you want to slam it shut. He has purple hair. Well, on one side. The other side is a greenish blue. He has about ten earrings in each ear and there appear to be more poking out of other parts of his body. I won't say where. You can almost see through his clothes, they're so tight, which might not be so bad except that you are pretty sure there is some type of weapon in his pocket. You would run screaming, only your dad is right behind you. You pray he won't let you go, but he does. On the date, every time you ask a question he sings his response. He has not spoken one word the whole evening. He doesn't wear shoes. Not your perfect date. Anyone here willing to describe what your perfect boyfriend or girlfriend would look like? (Allow students to answer. If no one does, ask if they could describe their worst nightmare of a date instead. Whatever you do, don't describe your perfect date.) Well, Jaime in *My Life as a Girl*, by Elizabeth Mosier, isn't that great at picking men. She goes off to a snobby rich college and her roommates are shocked when her "boyfriend" shows up. He is in cowboy boots and a hat. He knows how to line dance. And he steals cars. This is the perfect guy.

Myers, Walter Dean. 1999. *Monster.* New York: HarperCollins.
Realistic
Grades 7–10

There are tons of court shows on TV, real or fictional. There's Court TV, and big cases like O. J. Simpson's. And in *Monster*, by Walter Dean Myers, you can read the transcripts of Steve Harmon's case, knowing just as much as the jury, and decide for yourself whether or not you think he is guilty.

Paulsen, Gary. 1993. *Sisters/Hermanas*. San Diego: Harcourt Brace.
Short/Realistic/Spanish
Grades 8–11

You probably think that a prostitute and a cheerleader have nothing in common. (This introduction sometimes gets laughs or comments.) Or maybe you know some that do. But most of the time we think of them as two completely different people. And in *Sisters/Hermanas*, by Gary Paulsen, it goes back and forth. Tracy is a cheerleader. Her mom wants her to be the most popular girl in school, so she pays $3,000 for her to take these cheerleading lessons to make up this big routine for her. And on the other side, there is Rosa, who lives in a motel and can barely read English. And then one day they meet and find out that they are a little more alike than they would have thought.

Paulsen, Gary. 1995. *The Tent: A Parable in One Sitting*. San Diego: Harcourt Brace.
Short/Religious
Grades 6–9

All I can say about this book is that it is really short. There are wide spaces in between the lines and it is only 86 pages long. Basically, a father doesn't make much money and one night he steals a Bible from a motel room. He gets a huge tent with holes all over it from someone who owes him money, and he packs it all up into a truck to preach the word of God throughout the state and he drags his son with him to collect money. He had never even read the Bible before. Don't get any ideas from me.

Piven, Joshua, and David Borgenicht. 1999. *Worst Case Scenario Survival Handbook*. San Francisco: Chronicle Books.
Nonfiction/Humorous/Adult
Grades 9–12

Now this book is so useful. I mean, how many times have you been chased after through a building and don't know how to escape, or you have to get away from your crazy mom's driving or your brother and sister screaming, or even an intoxicated date, and wish you knew how to get out of the car, or you get a package and you're not sure if it is a surprise gift from your girlfriend or a bomb. *The Worst Case Scenario Survival Handbook* will help you out with all of those problems. There is a chapter of how to jump from a building into a dumpster, how to jump from a moving car, and even how to leap from a motorcycle to a car. It will show you how to identify a bomb, fend off a shark, escape from a sinking car, and win a sword fight, as well as escape from killer bees, wrestle free from an alligator, and deliver a baby in a cab. And there is even information on how to break into and hot-wire a car. In case you lose your keys, of course. I'm not promoting anything illegal here. This is everything you could possibly need to know before going to college (or high school). I wouldn't practice this, but you might want to read it just in case.

Pullman, Philip. 1997. *The Subtle Knife*. New York: Knopf.
Fantasy/Science Fiction
Grades 6–12

Let me see if I can read your minds. Any volunteers? Okay, now ask me any question you want me to try and answer about you that I wouldn't know and we'll see if I can do this. (Of course I fail.) Well, I'm not very good at this yet, but I wouldn't have to be if I lived in one of the three worlds in *The Subtle Knife*, by Phillip Pullman. It starts when a boy kills a man. It was self-defense, but the police are after him. When he runs away he accidentally finds the perfect hiding place—a hole in the air that leads him into another world that looks almost exactly like his own except there are no adults there. One of the girls he finds has this instrument that can answer any question and tell the truth. They find a knife that can cut through anything, even air. He has to find out what happened to his father and she has to find out why people are removing the animal that is a part of their bodies in her world.

Reid, Elwood. 1998. *If I Don't Six*. New York: Doubleday.
Sports/Realistic/Adult
Grades 11–12

Football and women. That's about all I can say about *If I Don't Six*, by Elwood Reid. And that's all college is really about anyway. Only when you have rules like no girls or parties, and the punishment for breaking these rules, which of course you would, is running the morning mile or getting beaten up by your teammates, it makes college and football not as much fun as expected.

Shusterman, Neal. 1997. *The Dark Side of Nowhere*. Boston: Little, Brown.
Science Fiction
Grades 6–8

You know how in the soap operas or those horror movies when you think someone is dead, but then you find out they were really just kidnapped or buried alive? In *The Dark Side of Nowhere*, by Neal Shusterman, a favorite classmate is now dead. The parents don't even cry at the funeral and they walk out as soon as they can. Jason thinks this is weird until he finds out that his friend is not dead. He has just turned into an alien who has come to invade the world, and Jason finds out that he will have to do the same thing.

Sleator, William. 1999. *Rewind.* New York: Dutton Children's Books.
Science Fiction
Grade 6–7

What are some times that you did something, or something so bad happened that you wish you could go back in time and change everything about that day? (If no one offers any suggestions, ask the following questions.) Did somebody tell someone else something you told them not to? Maybe about who you like? Did you get in trouble at school or at home? Well, in *Rewind,* by William Sleator, Peter gets a chance to do things over. He runs out into the street and is hit by a car, and finds that he has several chances to go back at any time he wants to try and change what happened so he won't run in front of that car again.

Soto, Gary. 1999. *Nerdlandia: A Play.* New York: PaperStar.
Play/Realistic
Grades 6–8

This one won't take you too long to read. It is a play, so there are lots of spaces in between the characters' lines. You don't really even have to read the stage instructions. That's just for if you were actually putting on the play. *Nerdlandia,* by Gary Soto, is about a nerd—Martin who wears his pants up to his chest, carries a calculator everywhere, and wears those taped up glasses. His friends want to make him cool so he can get with this girl Ceci who he's completely in love with. Meanwhile, of course Ceci is admitting to her friends that she has a huge crush on the nerd—Martin. Her friends take her to Nerdstroms so she can pick out a really nerdy outfit.

Stine, R. L. 1999. *Superstitious.* New York: Warner Books.
Suspense/Horror/Adult
Grades 9–12

I am sure none of you have ever thought about dating one of your teachers. For one thing it is illegal. But it happens. You hear it on the news all the time. But maybe none of that would ever happen if they had read *Superstitious*, by R. L. Stine—the adult book by the guy who wrote those *Goosebumps* books. Somehow people seem to die when this professor comes to teach at their school.

Stolz, Karen. 2000. *World of Pies*. New York: Hyperion.
Realistic/Historical Fiction/Adult
Grades 9–12

If you have to read a historical fiction book for class and are not into the Civil War or the Holocaust or medieval times, you might want to try *World of Pies*, by Karen Stolz. You might be able to get away with this one, since it is set in the '60s when a woman is almost not allowed to enter a pie-baking contest because she's black. And it is weird for the town to have a female mail carrier. You can throw in lots of stuff about equality there. Then one of the characters is sent to Vietnam where he loses an arm. There's your war. But it is really just the story of a girl growing up and meeting guys and dealing with her family and everyone's secrets in a small town.

Sykes, Shelly. 1998. *For Mike*. New York: Delacorte Press.
Mystery
Grades 7–8

Who is more important to you, your friend or your best friend? (The overall answer usually depends on who answers first.) Well, in *For Mike*, it is his best friend. He has been missing for three weeks. No one knows what happened to him. Then Jeff starts having these dreams where Mike appears to him with a bloody head and he's trying to tell him something and he has to figure out what it is.

Tangherlini, Arne E. 1999. *leo@fergusrules.com*. Wellfleet, Mass.: Leapfrog Press.
Fantasy/Science Fiction/Adult
Grades 8–12

You have probably heard stories about people pretending to be other people on the Internet to lure kids away from their home or to scam people out of their money. But sometimes people online pretend to be someone else to escape from a life they hate. Leo is short, has a big nose, and keeps getting kicked out of school. On the Internet she is beautiful and strong and no one knows what she is really like. In *leo@fergusrules.com*, Leo begins playing a virtual reality game in search of one of her friends. He is not her friend in real life, but in Apeiron, this virtual world or game, they can be different people. Anything can happen.

Thomas, Rob. 1997. *Doing Time: Notes from the Undergrad.* New York: Simon & Schuster.
Short Stories/Realistic
Grades 7–10

You probably have to do volunteer work for school or maybe you volunteer somewhere just to get some work experience. Or possibly just because you like it, right? (Don't expect them to agree. That is the point.) And maybe you dish out soup, or play games with the elderly, shelve books, or sort recyclables. But maybe, like the students at Robert E. Lee High in Rob Thomas's *Doing Time*, you find yourself delivering canned goods to your own home, live on the radio, or working with the hottest guy in school, even if he has a brain injury.

Tyree, Omar. 1996. *Flyy Girl.* New York: Simon & Schuster.
Realistic/Adult/College
Grades 11–12

I am sure the guys in the room have never done this, but let's pretend that you ask for this girl's phone number and then you never call her. And what would you do if this girl actually is brave enough to ask you why you never called. What would you say? (Wait for answers.) Okay, I think we have found out more than we need to know for now. Well, this particular girl in *Flyy Girl*, by Omar Tyree, is hot. She spends at least $500 a month on new clothes, more if you count the ones she gets guys to buy for her. She wears gold chains and earrings. And she has no problem telling people how "flyy" she thinks she is, turning down guys unless they look good and get into some kind of trouble. And she has a habit of picking liars for boyfriends. What does Victor tell her when she asks why he never called her? He comes up with "I just got back from shopping with my brother. He wouldn't let me use the car phone." Not bad, but if any of you guys decide to steal this excuse, I would say you were shopping with your mother instead. Girls like guys who are good to their mothers. She gets another lie from her new drug-dealing boyfriend named Cash Money. When he doesn't pick her up from school. His excuse: "Oh, this nut dude tried to get over on Wayne, so we had to smack 'im up a bit." OK maybe that one was real. At this point Tracy is not even 15 and she's been with about ten drug-dealing, lying, stealing, gun-carrying high school dropouts. Unlike any of you in this room, of course. But even after she moves on to college guys, she still wants the bad boys, even if they are in prison. There's also a sequel about when she gets older, called *For the Love of Money*.

Vail, Rachel. 1996. *Daring to Be Abigail*. New York: Orchard Books.
Realistic
Grade 6–7

How many of you have ever been to camp or camping? Or maybe even just to a sleepover? What are some of the tricks you might play on your friends? (Maybe they'll say the old hand in freezing water, freezing the bra, ghost outside the window, ketchup on their clothes, or you can offer some of these and more.) In *Daring to Be Abigail*, by Rachel Vail, not everyone at camp is as well liked as the others, so someone ends up with something you wouldn't want in your toothpaste.

Walter, Virginia. 1998. *Making Up Megaboy*. New York: DK.
Short/Realistic
Grades 6–8

OK, you get to school and your friend asks, "What book did you read for the book report?" You ask, "What book report?" He says, "The one that's due today, sixth period." You say a word I can't say in this classroom, run to the library, and find *Making Up Megaboy* which is only 62 pages long and really only half that length since every other page is a picture. It is about a boy who shoots a storeowner for no reason at all. Everyone he ever knew or never knew tells reporters and police what they think happened to Robbie. So you read it in between classes, slip it in your math book, type your report during lunch, and you are ready to hand it in during 6th. Maybe not an "A," but at least you're not failing the class.

Werlin, Nancy. 1998. *The Killer's Cousin*. New York: Delacorte Press.
Mystery
Grades 7–8

There was this guy in the news. He was charged with murder. He was let go. He didn't do it. But everyone still looks at him like he did. They see his face in the newspaper. Even his family. Relatives he was sent away to live with. He meets the cute girl. He meets the skinhead friend. He meets the psycho cousin. He meets his dead cousin. This is all in *The Killer's Cousin*, by Nancy Werlin.

Wittlinger, Ellen. 1999. *Hard Love*. New York: Simon & Schuster Books for Young Readers.
Realistic/Romance/Gay/Lesbian
Grades 7–9

Never fall in love. Especially if you know that person is not interested in you. Don't take the chance. I mean, you may be a great person. John in *Hard Love*, by Ellen Wittlinger, is a great writer. Not bad looking. He's funny. Will do anything you want him to, even go to see one of those Lilith Fair women singers. But if the girl, like Marisol, only wants to be friends, if she goes to the prom only to be polite, or if that girl only wants to actually date other girls, then you have no chance. You're not wonderful enough to change her mind *that* much. (You might want to follow up with a mention of the book *Breakup Girl to the Rescue!: A Superhero's Guide to Love and Lack Thereof*, by Lynn Harris.)

Wong, Janet S. 1999. *Behind the Wheel: Poems about Driving*. New York: Margaret K. McElderry Books.
Poetry
Grades 8–10

If you get a speeding ticket, you'll have to pay a huge fine or attend traffic school. If you get in an accident, you'll have to pay money. Your insurance will probably cover it, but maybe not. Instead, maybe a better insurance plan—insurance that would make sure you never got in an accident ever again—would be to stand in the middle of an intersection directing traffic all day. Then if you have a second offense, you'd have to direct the traffic with a shaved head right near your school parking lot. And after the third offense, you'd have to add singing in a microphone in pajamas with your parents. Or maybe you'd prefer that. I don't know. So if you ever need to read a book of poetry for school, and you read better than you drive, you might want to look at *Behind the Wheel*, by Janet S. Wong.

The World's Shortest Stories of Love and Death. 1999. Running Press.
Short Stories
Grades 9–12

Now let's say your teacher gives you an assignment to read a short story or a book of short stories. Now if he or she didn't say how short, then you should definitely try *The World's Shortest Stories of Love and Death*. They are all only 55 words long. That's not even a page. They're almost more like jokes than stories. Like this one—"Looking Ahead," by Cheryl L. Leflar.

> "In the woods. Alive."
> She gives the exact location.
> "Thank you!" The parents, in awe, rush from the room. The father pauses.
> "I'll leave your check on the table."
> The psychic nods.
> "That's fine. Now go to your child."
> He leaves. Another door opens.
> "What now?" a voice asks.
> "Snatch another kid," the psychic instructs.

I can't tell you about some of the other ones. (There are so many good ones in this book that you will have your pick or you can use a different one for different classes and see which ones get the best reaction. Some may go over the kids' heads if they don't have time to think about it—they won't be expecting the twists.)

Young, Karen Romano. 1999. *The Beetle and Me*. New York: Greenwillow Books.
Realistic
Grades 7–10

Guys, you're probably not going to find any girls in this room who can fix the engine of your car. Or maybe I'm wrong. Any girls in here ever change the oil? Let's back up. Anyone in this room ever drive? Well, Daisy in *The Beetle and Me* isn't old enough for a license yet either. (Use "Doesn't have her own car yet, either," if you are speaking to a high school group.) But she is determined to get the old VW Bug out of her garage and running without any help. Now maybe you'd rather your girlfriend was in the choir or on the basketball team. And some of the guys in this book think that way, too. Of course, it does impress some of the others. You just have to fix those cars and not care what those guys think of you. Or, of course, you could just read the book while they're doing all the work.

Zindel, Paul. 1998. *Reef of Death*. New York: HarperCollins.
Adventure/Horror/Mystery
Grades 6–8

You are probably lucky if your parents let you stay out until midnight. (Comments will arise on how much later or earlier they actually can stay out.) But for PC in *Reef of Death*, by Paul Zindel, his family is a little more adventurous. His uncle recruits PC to help him with money-making schemes in places like Costa Rica and the Yucatán, and his newest challenge is to go to Australia to find a treasure buried in the Great Barrier Reef. Only almost as soon as he arrives, his uncle is pulled into the water by a monster, swallowed, and chewed apart. And PC is left alone with the cute aboriginal girl to help her find their tribe's pearls buried long ago in the same water that killed his uncle and her brother.

Zindel, Paul. 1999. *Rats*. New York: Hyperion Books for Children.
Horror/Science Fiction
Grades 6–8

If you have ever been to Chicago and taken the El to "A Taste of Chicago" or the fireworks or the museum or something (use local city) then you might have been lucky enough to be staring down the tunnel, waiting for the lights of the train and instead see something moving on the tracks. Not your train, but rats. Chicago and New York have huge rat populations. Over seven million in New York. But at least they stay in your garbage and on the train tracks. Because they could, like in *Rats*, by Paul Zindel, show up in the toilet, hot tub, swimming pool, movie theater, water park, or your car. And instead of running by your feet, they might decide to eat them instead.

BOOKTALKS UTILIZING OTHER STYLES

The following booktalks by other librarians represent different styles and approaches from the ones I describe in this book.

Booktalk by John Sexton, Young Adult Librarian, Ashland Branch Library, Ashland, Oreg.

Almond, David. 2000. *Kit's Wilderness*. New York: Delacorte Press.
(This is an example of a longer talk with a more detailed plot description.)

It was just a game, but they called it "Death," and somehow that made it more than just a game. Maybe they called it Death because in the coal-mining town where they lived death was always present. It was there each day their fathers, their brothers, their grandfathers descended the shafts into the earth to dig for coal. Every single day, for as long as the mines had been there, death lurked in the shafts like some monster waiting to pounce and smother the town in clouds of grief. In a mining town you can't pretend that death will never happen to you or your family. You live in fear that it could happen any day. It had happened before. Accidents. Cave-ins. Death. For generations it had happened.

So when John Askew created this game he called Death, it seemed impossible for his classmates to resist the opportunity to experience for themselves the fear that their fathers knew. That their brothers knew. That their grandfathers knew. The fear that would someday be theirs when they descended into the mines.

The game was played in an abandoned part of the mines, in a cavern lit only by candles. The players sat in a circle. In the middle of the circle stood John Askew. He placed a long-bladed knife on the ground and looked around him.

"Whose turn is it to die?" he whispered, as he spun the knife. Whoever the blade pointed to when it stopped spinning would die that day.

"Death . . . Death . . . Death . . ." the group chanted as the knife spun. "Death . . . Death . . . Death . . ."

In the circle Kit Watson sat curious and fearful, feeling a chill each time the knife tip, glimmering in the candlelight, approached, then passed, approached, then passed his place in the circle. "Me . . . Not me . . . Me . . . Not me," thought Kit. And then, finally, "Me," as the blade came to a stop pointing directly at him.

Askew took him to the center of the circle. There were tears in Kit's eyes and he was trembling. He heard giggles around the circle. Did the others think he was chicken, or were they just glad it wasn't them about to play this game of Death? Looking into Askew's eyes, Kit Watson recited the words he was told, words that softened his fear, words that transformed Askew's eyes into long, dark tunnels down which Kit felt himself drawn deeper and deeper and deeper. There was no pretending now . . . Kit felt that he would truly die. And then, finally, he was no more!

What will Kit experience as he is left alone in the depths of the dark game called "Death"? Discover what the eternal darkness holds for him when you read *Kit's Wilderness*, by David Almond.

Booktalk by Stephanie A. Squicciarini, MLS graduate student, SUNY–Buffalo.

Lowry, Lois. 1993. *The Giver*. Boston: Houghton Mifflin.
(This booktalk is more of a game to allow students to participate.)

Before we begin, I want you to think when you were a child and what you always dreamed of being when you grew up. Keep that in the back of your mind. Now, I want to welcome you to a world with no hunger, a world with no pain, no war, a world where everyone has a specific role that creates a place that knows only happiness. Anyone that may jeopardize that happiness and peace, anyone that does not seem fit enough to handle their role will be quietly released. What does that mean, quietly released . . . well very few people know.

Tonight we will assign roles to ten children who will now be adults. This is the Ceremony of Twelve. We have completed the Ceremony of Eight where our Sevens became old enough to get new jackets with smaller buttons and pockets for the very first time. Our Ceremony of Nine where the new Nines received their bicycles. And our Ceremony of Ten where children received identifying haircuts, girls losing their braids and boys losing their childish locks.

But the Ceremony of Twelve is most important. The assignments our Twelves receive now will stay with them forever. The Committee of Elders has made countless observations to ensure that these assignments are fitting of the child, now adult. I will call each new Twelve one by one in the order that they were born twelve years ago. Could each of you stand as I call your number and then be seated once you are told your assignment.

Number 1: You will be a Sanitation Laborer
Number 2: You will be a Nurturer
Number 3: You will be a Speaker
Number 4: You will be a Caretaker of Old
Number 6: You will be a Birth Mother
Number 7: You will be an Engineer
Number 8: You will be a Fish Hatchery Attendant
Number 9: You will be a Director of Recreation
And Number 10: You will be an Instructor of Threes

Now many of you have probably noticed that I skipped number 5. I assure you there has been no mistake and I am sorry for causing you anxiety. Our #5, can you please stand up. Jonas, you have been chosen to be assigned the most respected and most important role in our community. We have taken our time in selecting Jonas for this assignment as we all know what happened last time. We could not afford another failure. Jonas, you have been selected for a role that requires Intelligence, Integrity, Courage, and Wisdom. But most of all, you have been selected because we believe you have the Capacity to See Beyond. For these reasons you have been selected to be the next Receiver of Memory. This is the most crucial role for our community and you can take the journey to discover what all this means with Jonas in Lois Lowry's book, *The Giver*. When you hear that #5 is skipped over, could you please whisper to your neighbor: "Hey wait, she skipped #5!"

When you hear that #5 is skipped over, could you please whisper to your neighbor: "Why do you think she skipped #5!"

When you hear that #5 is skipped over, could you please whisper to your neighbor: "Oh no! She skipped #5!"

When you hear that #5 is skipped over, could you please whisper to your neighbor: "Why do you think she skipped #5!"

When you see #5 stand up, could you please shift in your seat.
When you see #5 stand up, could you please shift in your seat.
When you see #5 stand up, could you please shift in your seat.
When you see #5 stand up, could you please shift in your seat.

Booktalk by Lori Hodges Fritz, College Station Public Library, College Station, Tex.

Beattie, Owen, and John Geiger. 1992. *Buried in Ice*. New York: Scholastic.
(Here nonfiction is used to interest readers.)

What does a human body look like when it has been buried in ice for 140 years? This is just one of the questions Owen Beattie and John Geiger are able to answer after they unearth the bodies of three sailors who died on an ill-fated quest for the Northwest Passage.

Captain John Franklin and his two ships, the Erebus and the Terror, set sail from England on May 19, 1845, in hopes of finding a route north of Canada to the Pacific Ocean. The ships and their crews were never seen again.

What could possibly have happened to make two ships and 134 crewmen disappear into thin air? This is just what Owen Beattie and John Geiger hope to find out as they dig up the bodies that have been for so long *Buried in Ice*.

Booktalks by Joel Shoemaker, School Media Specialist, Iowa City, Iowa.

(Joel does not write his booktalks. Instead, he reviews his notes to familiarize himself with the names of characters and key points. He may mark critical passages with sticky notes. Then, with an opening sentence in mind, he talks informally, using the audience response to determine what to expand on.)

Bauer, Cat. 2000. *Harley, Like a Person*. Delray Beach, Fla.: Winslow Press.

Ever had the feeling that you must be adopted 'cause these people can't possibly be your parents? Harley (no, not like the motorcycle—like a person) has always thought her abusive and alcoholic parents were hiding something. She finds a clue, a note written to her when she was an infant that's not in her dad's handwriting, but it's written as if it's her dad! She must be on to something, right? She's like a detective, piecing together her own story, finding evidence that will prove she's right. Won't it?

Efaw, Amy. 2000. *Battle Dress*. New York: HarperCollins.

Andi is a talented, smart, athletic new cadet immersed in West Point's summer camp, appropriately named, "The Beast." Constant pressure to conform, to compete, to excel in the classroom and field exercises wears and tests and tears her down. But the secret she guards is that this is easy compared to being home. She's got to make it here, because she's not going back there for anything.

Klass, David. 2001. *You Don't Know Me*. Farrar, Straus & Giroux.

It's hard to get to know John, who is 14 years old, plays the tuba in band, and is sure he's in love with Gloria, the most beautiful girl in the world. It's hard for anyone to get to know him because he does not want to let you or anyone else get to know him. He hides a lot of things from not only you, the reader, but also from his mom, the kids at school, and his teachers. Sometimes he hides behind outrageous, sarcastic humor, other times behind troublemaking at school. But behind it all is the father who is not his father, and the threats he makes, and the beatings he delivers.

McNichols, Ann. 2000. *Falling from Grace*. New York: Walker.

In 1929 there was moonshine liquor, the Ku Klux Klan was riding and burning, and Cassie sees her daddy, "the banker," carrying on with the preacher's wife. No wonder her big sister, Adra, ran away that Sunday, but she and her momma are still there to deal with it all.

Spinelli, Jerry. 2000. *Stargirl*. New York: Alfred A. Knopf.

Leo, best friend Kevin, and the rest of their classmates in Mica, Arizona, are stunned by the appearance of Stargirl, a new student who wears weird clothes, serenades them with her ukelele in the lunchroom, and joins the cheerleading squad but cheers for both sides equally. At first she seems to be winning them over, and Leo and Stargirl fall in love. But that cheerleading thing, cheering for the enemy—now Leo and Stargirl are shunned, left out of everything, ignored, despised. To thine own self be true, or be true to your school? What do you you think would happen if there was a character like Stargirl in our school?

Booktalks by Rebecca Purdy.

Abraham, Pearl. 1996. *The Romance Reader*. New York: Riverhead
Books.
(This first booktalk is in the form of a list. Students will be angered be-
fore they even know why.)

Girls can't sing.
Girls can't wear bathing suits in front of boys.
When a woman gets married she must shave her head and keep it
shaved. She may wear a wig or a kerchief. No Hassidic Jew can ride in
a car or touch money on Shabbat, the Sabbath.
Rachel's father wears short pants that tie just below his knees.
She has to wear tights and long sleeves all year, even in July.
She's expected to enter into an arranged marriage, never work, and
never see the world
And worse for Rachel she's not allowed to read goyim books, books
written by non-Jews. That means none of those romances she loves.
Rachel loves her family even though her father embarrasses her and
her mother is always angry, but she doesn't know if she can do what they
want and keep

Cochran, Thomas. 1997. *Roughnecks*. San Diego: Harcourt Brace.
(Boys will appreciate the emphasis on the importance of football.)

Winners and losers. Football is king in Oil Camp. When baby boys are
born they are given a miniature football in the hospital. Townspeople
take off work to go to the pep rallies. They never miss a game. This town
is all about winning.
And in Oil Camp, Travis Cody is famous for two things. First he's a
great football player. Second, he's the reason the Oil Camp Roughnecks
don't have an undefeated season. He blew one play against Jericho
Grooms of the Pineview Pelicans and that's all it took. His team lost,
no, his town lost, and it was his entire fault.
Now it's the day of the big game. The Louisiana AA State High School
Football Championship. And they'll all be watching—the whole town.
His brother, his girlfriend, everyone he knows. They'll all be waiting to
see if he's a winner or a loser.

Booktalk by Jennifer Maria Collins, Teen Outreach Librarian, San Francisco Public Library.

LL Cool J with Karen Hunter. 1997. *I Make My Own Rules*. New York: St. Martin's Press.

(Using a popular celebrity is a great way to present a talk. It sounds as if the booktalker is knowledgeable about one of their favorite people and will pay attention to find the facts that they don't know. Just be careful that the person you select is still popular with your teenagers.)

One rule that LL Cool J made for himself for a long time was to never take his hat off. And most people have respected that. But when LL Cool J met somebody more famous than himself, he was forced to break that rule. He was invited to Bill Cosby's house for dinner, and as he came into the entrance of the house, Mr. Cosby said, "What are you doing in my house with your hat on?" Then he ordered LL Cool J to take the hat off. But Cool J didn't even do his hair at that time because he was always wearing a hat. Still, he felt that he had to respect Bill Cosby's wishes, so he took the hat off, and sat down at the dining room table, and sat there with his hair looking crazy. All the guests were trying not to laugh at him, until finally, Mr. Cosby said, "put your hat back on." Then, everybody laughed.

Cool J will tell you what drove him to wear a hat all the time. It wasn't something he just started doing when he became a successful rap artist. Since he was a teenager, he'd been wearing a hat almost constantly. It wasn't something his parents told him to do. His mother was too busy working. And his father wasn't around, ever since he shot Cool J's mother and grandfather in front of a very young Cool J. There was another influence in LL Cool J's life, someone cruel and hateful, who made him lose his sense of who he was, and rap was one of the few things that could help him get back to knowing his true self. But he had a long road ahead of him.

Part III

Booktalking Resources

BACKTALKING SOURCES CITED IN THIS BOOK

Bodart, Joni. 1985. *Booktalk 2: Booktalking for All Ages and Audiences*. New York: H. W. Wilson.

Bodart, Joni. 1987. *The Effect of a Booktalk Presentation of Selected Titles on the Attitude Toward Reading of Senior High School Students and on the Circulation of These Titles in the High School Library*. Denton, Tex.: Texas Woman's University.

Bromann, Jennifer. 1999. "The Toughest Audience on Earth." *School Library Journal*. (October): 60-63.

Edwards, Margaret. 1994. *The Fair Garden and the Swarm of Beasts: The Library and the Young Adult*. Chicago: American Library Association.

Gillespie, John, and Diana Lembo. 1967. *Juniorplots: A Book Talk Manual for Teachers and Librarians*. New York: R. R. Bowker.

Gillespie, John T., and Corinne J. Naden. 1989. *Seniorplots: A Book Talk Guide for Use with Readers Ages 15–18*. New York: R. R. Bowker.

Jones, Patrick. 1998. *Connecting Young Adults and Libraries: A How-To-Do-It Manual*, 2d ed. New York: Neal-Schuman.

Keane, Nancy. "Booktalks Quick and Simple." *http://rms.concord.k12.nj.us/booktalks/* (February 2001).

Littlejohn, Carol. 2000. *Keep Talking That Book!: Booktalks to Promote Reading Volume II*. Worthington, Ohio: Linworth Publishing.

Munson, Amelia H. 1950. *An Ample Field: Books and Young People*. Chicago: American Library Association.

Polette, Nancy, ed. 1994. *Novel Booktalks to Read and Perform: Readers Theatre Booktalks*. O'Fallon, Mo.: Book Lures.

Rochman, Hazel. 1987. *Tales of Love and Terror: Booktalking the Classics, Old and New*. Chicago: American Library Association.

Vaillancourt, Renée J. 2000. *Bare Bones Young Adult Services: Tips for Public Library Generalists*. Chicago: American Library Association.

ELECTRONIC MAILING LISTS

The following electronic mailing lists deal specifically or occasionally with
booktalking to young adults. Information on subscribing can be found
on the Web sites.

Booktalkers. *www.yahoogroups.com*
Booktalking. *www.yahoogroups.com*
TAGAD. *www.topica.com*
YALSA-BK. *www.ala.org/yalsa/*

Index
By Subject, Title, and Author

Index
By Genre and Theme

About the Author

Jennifer Bromann is head of youth services at the Prairie Trails Public Library in Burbank, IL. She received her undergraduate degree from the University of Illinois-Champaign/Urbana in rhetoric and the teaching of English before pursuing library and information science at the University of Wisconsin-Milwaukee, and is completing her certification in school media at Dominican University in River Forest, IL. She has worked in a school, two law firm libraries, and public libraries. Her first article, "The Toughest Audience on Earth" was published in *School Library Journal* in October 1999. Jennifer has presented workshops on literature for middle and high school readers as well as on booktalking. She continues to write and present on teen and library issues. She can be contacted at *bromannj@hotmail.com*.